DEVON
NARROW GAUGE

Maurice Dart

Series editor Vic Mitchell

MP Middleton Press

Cover pictures:

*Front left - On 29th August 1999 0-4-2T **Denzil** is running around its train at Cape of Good Hope Halt on the Exmoor Steam Railway. A line of 2ft gauge ex South African Railways Beyer Garratts were behind the hedge in the workshop yard. (M.Dart)*

*Front right - On 30th December 2006 0-6-0WT **Bronllwyd** awaits departure from Woody Bay on the Lynton & Barnstaple Railway with a train to the newly opened terminus at Killington Lane. (M.Dart)*

*Back - The author stands beside Hunslet 0-4-4-0 diesel **Carnegie** at Bicton station on the Bicton Woodland Railway on 23rd June 1997. (Mrs R.Barrett)*

Published July 2007

ISBN 978 1 906008 09 3

© Middleton Press, 2007

Design Deborah Esher

Published by
       Middleton Press
       Easebourne Lane
       Midhurst
       West Sussex
       GU29 9AZ
Tel: 01730 813169
Fax: 01730 812601
Email: info@middletonpress.co.uk
www.middletonpress.co.uk

Printed & bound by Biddles Ltd, Kings Lynn

CONTENTS

1. Industry

1	Dewerstone Tramway, Shaugh Bridge
2	ECC Ball Clays, Meeth
3	Fatherford Tramway, Okehampton
4	Hey Tor Granite Tramway
6	Lundy North Light Tramway
8	Lundy Quarry Railway
11	Meldon Tramways
12	North Devon Clay Co Ltd, Peters Marland
22	Plymouth & Dartmoor Railway - Lee Moor Tramway
55	Redlake Railway
60	Shaugh Iron Mine Tramway, Shaugh Bridge
61	Sidmouth Harbour Railway
62	Westleigh Quarry, Burlescombe

I.   This map shows the locations of the systems that are included in this album in relation to the principal main line railways. North is at the top of all maps. (M.Dart/S.Parkinson)

2. Military

63	Efford Fort, Plymouth
65	Froward Point, Kingswear
68	Okehampton Range Target Railways
72	RNAD Ernesettle, Plymouth

3. Main Line Owned

73	Lynton & Barnstaple Railway

4. Tourist

80	Bicton Woodland Railway, Budleigh Salterton
83	C.Burges, Christow Station
85	Devon Railway Centre, Cadeleigh Station
89	Exmoor Steam Railway, Bratton Fleming
94	Lynbarn Light Railway, near Clovelly
98	Lynton & Barnstaple Railway
111	Lynton & Lynmouth Cliff Railway
114	Morwellham Quay Mine Tramway
119	Powderham Castle Railway

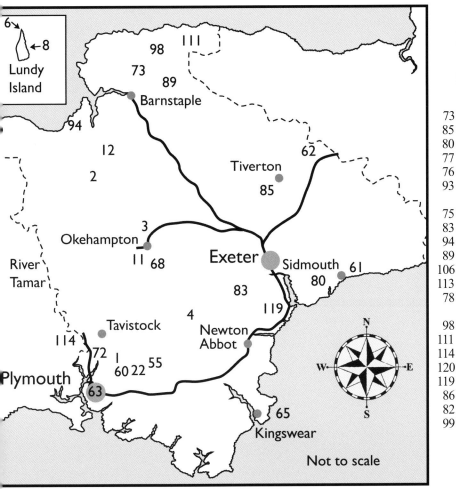

INDEX TO PUBLIC STATIONS

73	Barnstaple Town
85	Bickleigh
80	Bicton
77	Blackmoor Gate
76	Bratton Fleming
93	Cape of Good Hope Halt
75	Chelfham
83	Christow
94	Downland Cross
89	Exmoor Town
106	Killington Lane
113	Lynmouth
78	Lynton L & B Rly (Original line)
98	Lynton L & B Rly
111	Lynton L & L Rly
114	Morwellham
120	Old Smithy
119	Powderham Castle
86	Riverside Halt
82	The Hermitage
99	Woody Bay

ACKNOWLEDGEMENTS

I am most grateful to all of the photographers and others, whose names are included with the captions, for providing material for use in this book. I extend my thanks to C.Bristow, Lieutenant Colonel A.H.Clark, M.Daly, Dr T.Greeves, R.Hateley, S.Jenkins, The Landmark Trust, N.Langridge, S.Parkinson, Mrs V.Quickley, T.Rouse, K.Searle, Mrs G.Searle, T.Stanbury, D.Tooke and Mrs R.Wilson. My thanks are also extended to the China Clay History Society for access to and permission to use photographs from their archive. I would also like to thank the Curator and staff at the Westcountry Library at Exeter and Okehampton Library for their help with maps and information. I also extend my thanks to G.L.Crowther for permission to reproduce sections of some of his maps from his *National Atlas Showing Canals, Navigable Rivers, Mineral Tramroads, Railways and Street Tramways; Volume 7d – Devon*. I also thank the management and staff at the preserved railways which are included in the book for providing me with facilities for photography and Mr & Mrs Stirland of the Exmoor Steam Railway for a track layout diagram and permitting a private visit to their establishment.

INTRODUCTION

Mention the County of Devon and one usually thinks about red cliffs and golden sandy beaches, the two high moors, or the cities of Plymouth and Exeter. However, in the past centuries, the high moors have been home to numerous quarries. Also, rivers thread their way down rich alluvial valleys, to carry the rainfall from the moors to the sea. In many of these valleys metallic deposits were formed on the outside of the central backbone of the moors. These deposits have been exploited over the years and gave rise to a large number of mines producing ores of a variety of metals. Almost every quarry and mine possessed its own tramway, many being very short in length. Some of them carried ore from the mine to loading points on the rivers, whilst others carried stone to crushing and grading plants and then to similar loading points. With the arrival of standard gauge railways, tramways were constructed to deliver the raw material to conveniently placed loading points by sidings. So, all over the county, various industrial lines developed. Some lasted only for short periods and these, with many of the others, were rarely photographed. Dartmoor has provided an excellent training ground for the military for many years and, near Plymouth and around the coast, various military defences and munitions depots have been established. Most of these establishments possessed narrow gauge lines, but they were generally 'off limits' to the general public and so few photographs exist of these locations. North Devon possessed the narrow gauge Lynton & Barnstaple Railway which was, in effect, a main line railway. Latterly, it was owned later by the SR. Prior to the 1970s there were very few tourist lines in the county, but these have multiplied over the last few decades, and are mainly found around the coastal holiday centres and at tourist attractions. Some of these are still undergoing expansion. One military line, for which no photos have been located, that deserves mention, is the 1ft 6in gauge internal system that served the MOD depot at Bullpoint, Plymouth. This system operated from the early 1920s until 1958. Similarly, no photos have come to light of the locos or lines at Wilminstone Quarry, near Tavistock. As there is a separate volume by Middleton Press devoted to the Seaton Electric Tramway, the line is not included in this book. The original Lynton & Barnstaple Railway, together with the Lynton & Lynmouth Cliff Railway, have also been the subjects of a separate book by this publisher. But as fresh photos are to hand, a representative selection is included for each of them. The reopening of a section of the Lynton & Barnstaple Railway, with further extensions planned has considerably heightened interest in this area of the county.

1. Industry

DEWERSTONE TRAMWAY, SHAUGH BRIDGE

Planned by the South Devon & Tavistock Railway, the Dewerstone Tramway was owned by the Hey Tor Granite Co and was intended to link the quarries with the Tavistock branch line near Goodameavy, north of Shaugh tunnel. A standard gauge line climbed east and then south from the east bank of the River Mewy. It passed over a bridge across the Blacklands Brook, to reach a loading and transfer point in Dewerstone Woods. There was a subsidiary quarry here, and the base of a crane exists. From here, narrow gauge rails, probably of 2ft gauge, climbed north east for 400yd on a 1 in 6 counterbalanced incline, to a second reversing point, where the winding drum house was positioned. On the incline, double lines were carried on three runs of granite setts. From the reversing point the line ran south to the main quarry, the face of which was 45ft high. The line continued west to spoil tips. One abutment and one pier were built for the proposed bridge to cross the River Mewy, but it was not completed, so no standard gauge wagons ever crossed the river. The line, which was around one mile in total length, was built in 1858 and operated for around twenty years.

II. *The line of the tramway has been drawn in on combined sections of adjacent OS maps of 1907. Both reversing points are shown, with the straight inclined section between them.* **(OS/M.Dart)**

(insert) 1. *The derelict winding drum in the remains of the drumhouse at the top of the incline, are seen during the 1920s.* **(M.Dart coll.)**

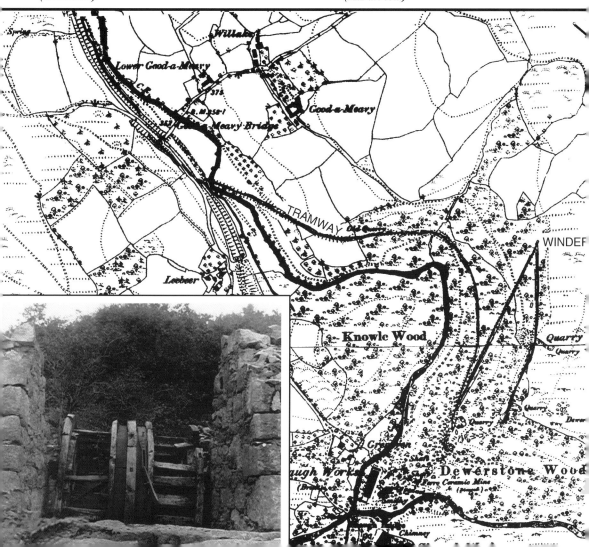

ECC BALL CLAYS, MEETH

The Meeth (North Devon) Clay Co Ltd opened a works with drying sheds to extract ball clay from pits in the area. When the Southern Railway line from Halwill to Torrington opened in 1925, a siding was laid to connect the line to the drying sheds. A system of 2ft gauge lines connected several mines to the drying sheds. From 1967 the works was owned by Hexter & Budge, and was part of the ECC group. It became part of ECC Ball Clays Ltd in August 1970. From 1967 extensive opencast mines were developed and, from 1968, road vehicles became the mode of transport to the drying sheds, and the internal railway system fell out of use. By August 1970 most of the equipment and track had been removed.

III.   The course of the tramway has been drawn on this 1 inch OS map of 1927. It is shown running south west a little to the north of Meeth. The line from Dunsbear to Peters Marland works, and across Marland Moor, also appears on the map. (OS/M.Dart)

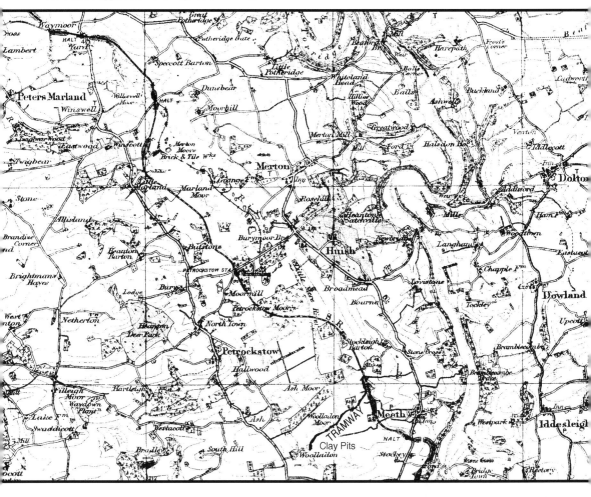

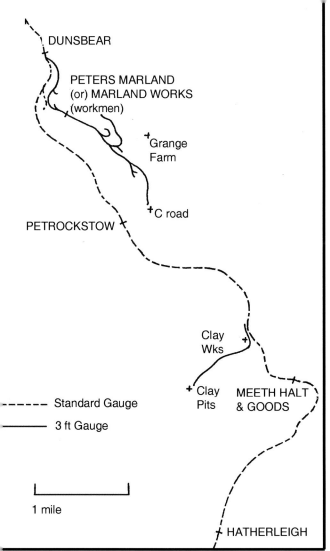

DUNSBEAR

PETERS MARLAND
(or) MARLAND WORKS
(workmen)

+ Grange
Farm

+ C road

PETROCKSTOW +

Clay
Wks

+ Clay   MEETH HALT
Pits   & GOODS

- - - - - Standard Gauge

———— 3 ft Gauge

|——————|
1 mile

+ HATHERLEIGH

IV.   This diagram shows the relative positions of both systems clearly. (L.Crowther)

Further photographs appear in Middleton Press album Branch Lines To Torrington.

2.   One of the Ruston & Hornsby diesel locos stands inside one of the drying sheds on 20th March 1965. This was works no.237897 and was built in 1945. Numerous pieces of ball clay lie on the drying floor behind the loco. (R.Hateley)

FATHERFORD TRAMWAY

The contractor, Robert T.Relf, was responsible for constructing the railway line from Okehampton Road (Sampford Courtney) to Lidford (Lydford) for the Devon & Cornwall Railway, which became part of the LSWR. To obtain stone for the construction of bridges and viaducts, a narrow gauge tramway was built from a quarry at Fatherford, southward for around seven eighths of a mile to the site of Okehampton station. The gauge of this horse-worked line, which opened in 1870, is not quoted in any reference sources. The line commenced just southwest of the up side of Okehampton station, and ran parallel to the main line and gradually dropped to pass below Fatherford Viaduct to access the quarry. The tramway and quarry remained in use, and during the First World War timber was carried to Okehampton station. It was subsequently closed, and the rails were lifted during the1930s. Today, the route is used as a footpath, and is locally referred to as 'The Old Tram Lines'.

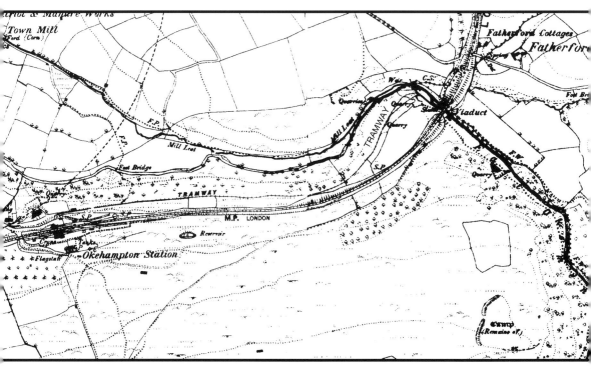

V. *The quarry is on the right of this 1888 OS map produced at 6ins to 1 mile.*

3. *Despite extensive searching, no photos have been discovered showing trains, or even rails, on this line. So this, one view, is included to show the general scene. Taken on 23rd July 1994 we are mid-way from Fatherford Quarry to Okehampton station, looking west up the rising gradient. In this section, the line ran on a ledge with ground descending to the valley on the north side. Earth and stone walls border the route on the east side. (M.Dart)*

HEY TOR GRANITE TRAMWAY

The Hey Tor Granite Co laid a tramway to connect quarries around Hey Tor (now Haytor) Rock to the Stover Canal at Teignrace. The rails and sleepers were granite and the 4ft 3in gauge line which ran for seven miles, opened on 16th September 1820. At the Hey Tor end, spur lines served Emsworthy Rocks east and west quarries, Holwell quarry, Hey Tor quarry, and a rubble heap. When the Moretonhampstead & South Devon Railway constructed their line, they used 2 ¼ miles of the trackbed of the Hey Tor line from Teignrace to Pottery Pool. Exchange of traffic took place at Granite siding, south of Bovey station. The line climbed a total of 1400 ft. and fell out of regular use by 1858, but probably saw sporadic use for a further twenty years. Much of the track can still be found in situ. Horses were used to work open sided tramroad trucks, which it has been suggested may have been converted from road wagons.

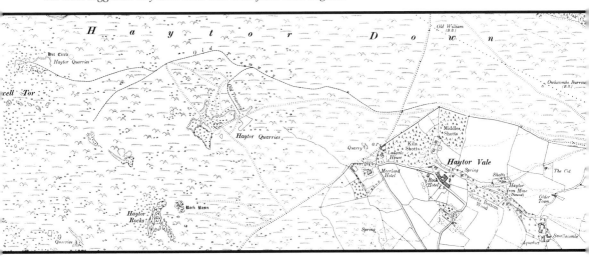

VI.   The truncated line of the tramway with branch lines to several quarries is shown on this OSmap of 1907, which is at a reduced scale.

VII.   Parts of two sections of diagrammatic maps have been joined to show the original full extent of the line. (L.Crowther)

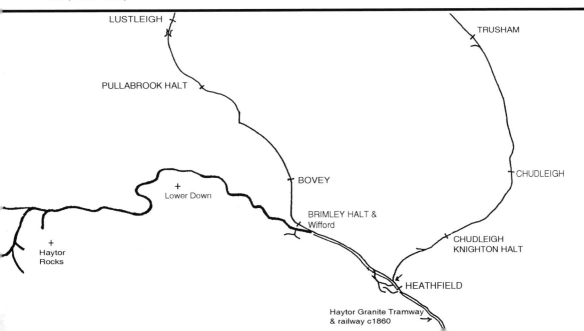

4.   *Here we look north east at a granite point, which formed the junction of routes from two quarries. Hey Tor is behind the photographer. This scene was recorded during a visit by Plymouth Railway Circle on 20th June 1965. Fellow member Larry Crosier is standing on the overgrown trackbed. (M.Dart)*

5.   *This view, taken during the same visit, shows granite rails along the route which led north east from No. 2 Quarry. Note the large pieces of granite which border the route. (M.Dart)*

LUNDY NORTH LIGHT TRAMWAY

A lighthouse was constructed at the north end of Lundy Island in 1897. As only a rough track existed from the landing beach up to the village and along the centre of the top of the island to the north end, supplies were delivered to the lighthouse by boat. They were winched up from the boat to a level area from where a 2ft gauge, manually worked tramway, ran for several hundred yards to the lighthouse. The lighthouse became automated during the 1980s and the tramway fell out of use, but most of the rails still remain.

6.   This view, which looks east from the lighthouse along the tramway, was taken on 7th September 2005. In the distance where the line curves to the left, the structure on the right was the base of a winch that was used to haul supplies up from boats below. Power for the winch was supplied by the cable secured to the line of supports on the left side of the track. (M.Dart)

7.   Now we see the end of the line at the spot where supplies were winched up from boats. The base of the winch is on the left as we look west to the lighthouse on 7th September 2005. (M.Dart)

LUNDY QUARRY RAILWAY

The Lundy Granite Company was registered in July 1863 and was wound up in November 1868. It operated five quarries on the east side of the island between the Quarter and Halfway Walls, and a railway, believed to be of 2ft gauge, was laid to serve them. Wooden sleepers about 4ft 3in long were spaced roughly 3ft apart. Lines from the top quarry ran south west to spoil tips. The top quarry was 80ft above a two line marshalling area, to which it was connected by an incline which had a gradient of 1 in 2½. This quarry is flooded, and is known as 'The Black Pool'. From the marshalling area, now called 'The Terrace', a line ran north, gradually climbing along the side of the island for one third of a mile to serve four other quarries. The quarries were accessed by short lines, which ran to spoil tips above the sea. These lines crossed the main line by turntables. Another line descended from the marshalling area on a gradient of 1 in 1½ to Quarry Beach from where a line ran to a loading area which consisted of a granite quay with a wooden jetty. The marshalling area was 260ft above sea level. The company owned a 35 hp, 56 ton steam tug called **The Vanderbyl**, which was built in 1864. This vessel regularly transported stone to Fremington Quay, for onward transit by main line railway. When the Quarry Company ceased trading, the rails were lifted but indentations where sleepers were laid are still apparent.

VIII. This map shows the full extent of the quarry railway with details of the inclines and other gradients. (K.Gardner/ The Landmark Trust)

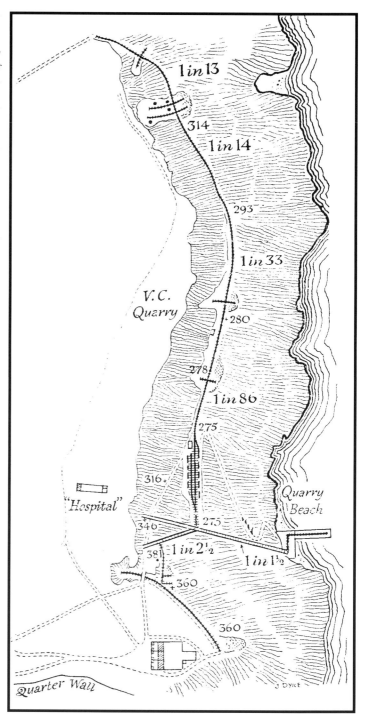

8.   *Unusual to be included in this series of books, is a scene from the distant past. It is displayed in the small museum on Lundy and is included, as only the trackbed remains today. In the foreground is the storage and cutting shed for the quarries, two of which are in the distance. Beyond those the railway curved left following the coast to serve two other quarries. A derrick for loading stone into wagons is at each quarry, and the lines leading to spoil tips on the cliff edge are shown. At the bottom of the picture are the two circular pits that housed the winding drums from where cables led across a trough to the incline, which descended to Quarry Beach. Blocks of granite are being loaded onto one of the trolleys, ready to descend. (The Landmark Trust)*

9.   Here we look from near the top quarry on 7 th September 2005 to the area depicted in the previous scene. The works area remains as an open space with a border of pieces of granite. The route to the quarries heads north along the top of the cliffs. A spoil tip, from the nearest quarry, descends from the trackbed. (M.Dart)

10.   At the south end of the marshalling area, the circular granite pits that housed the winding drums for the incline, together with the trough which the cables passed across, was recorded on 7 th September 2005. (M.Dart)

MELDON TRAMWAYS

Copper was mined in the valley of the West Okement River in the area below Meldon viaduct in the early 1800s, but the mine closed down after a few years. It re-opened in 1863 as the Devon Copper Mine and a short tramway probably existed to serve the mine, which finally closed in 1865. Limestone quarries had existed in the valley in the early 1800s, but were completely abandoned by 1808. These works had re-opened by the 1840s and kilns were built on each side of the river. A large quarry on the west bank of the river was connected to the kiln by a narrow gauge tramway, which also ran south over a bridge and climbed an incline to end near the modern reservoir. The quarry on the east side of the river fell out of use in the 1880s when aplite quarries were opened on the same and nearby sites. The limestone quarry on the west bank of the river operated until at least the end of the nineteenth century, but a precise date of closure has not been found. Aplite, also known as Granulite, was mined on the east side of the river and the area worked occupied land on the north and south sides of the Red-a-Ven Brook which was a tributary of the river. This ore was used in the production of green glass and a glass bottle works was established to serve chemist shops in the surrounding locality. A line ran north from the mine to the bottle works and continued north to serve waste dumps. Another line ran south and climbed to an area near the entrance to the well-known stone quarry, to deliver supplies to the works and to transport finished bottles outwards. Operations ceased during the 1920s but trackbeds, bridge abutments, finger tips and dumps remain to be explored, together with a bridge over the river which carried a line for a period. From examination of views which show the Aplite works, the gauge of the tramway would appear to have been 2ft.

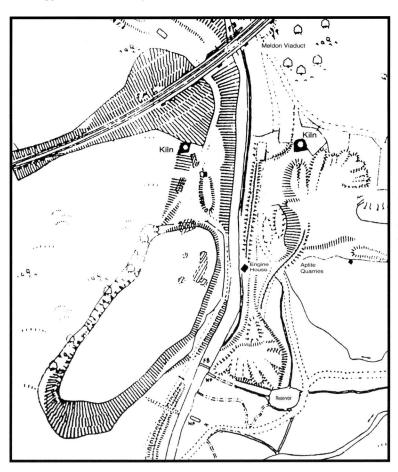

IX. **This OS map of 1888 has the aplite quarries on the east bank of the river. One line is shown curving to quarries. Another line runs north by the river bank from the engine house to the tip truck shed. On the west bank, one tramway runs near the river south of the limestone quarry. Another line runs west up an incline from a point adjacent to the footbridge over the river. It is suspected that at one period, a line crossed this bridge to link the systems.**

11.   *This scene looks north down the valley of the West Okement River with Meldon Viaduct straddling the valley. On the left (west) bank, a large lime kiln can be seen. A tramway led to the top of the kiln to feed the limestone in. The Aplite works are on the right bank. Three lines lead from the cutting sheds. The nearest route leads north, along the river bank to quarrying areas behind the camera. A line leads across the centre of the picture, to a quarry, whilst a third line curves sharply, and passes through a gate towards the glass works. (M.Dart coll.)*

⟶ *Ball clay has been mined in the area around Peters Marland since at least 1850 and in 1875, W.A.B.Wren was responsible for the workings. On 12th December 1879 the Marland Brick & Clay Works was incorporated to operate the brickworks until 1888, but the North Devon Clay Co controlled clay extraction. On 1st May 1880 a contract was let to the Green Odd Railway & General Contracting Co Ltd which was owned by the famous J.B.Fell, to construct the 3ft gauge Marland Light Railway. It was to run from clay workings on Marland and Merton Moors to Torrington to carry clay to the main line station. The first train ran on 1st January 1881. When the North Devon & Cornwall Junction Light Railway opened on 27th July 1925, this line used 4½ miles of the 3ft gauge route from Torrington. A siding from the new line ran to the works, from where a network of 3ft gauge lines continued in use to access the clay mines. A 'Workmens' service had operated on the 3ft gauge line between Torrington and Marland. During 1970 the mines were gradually abandoned in favour of opencast workings, linked to the processing works by internal roadways. Road transport replaced the 3ft gauge lines and the last train carrying clay operated on 13th November 1970, with all of the track being removed on 11/12th December following. The standard gauge lines closed to all traffic on 12th September 1982.*

NORTH DEVON CLAY COMPANY LTD
PETERS MARLAND

Further photos appear in
Branch Lines to Torrington.

X. The OS 1 inch map of 1919 shows the entire length of the Torrington & Marland Light Railway.

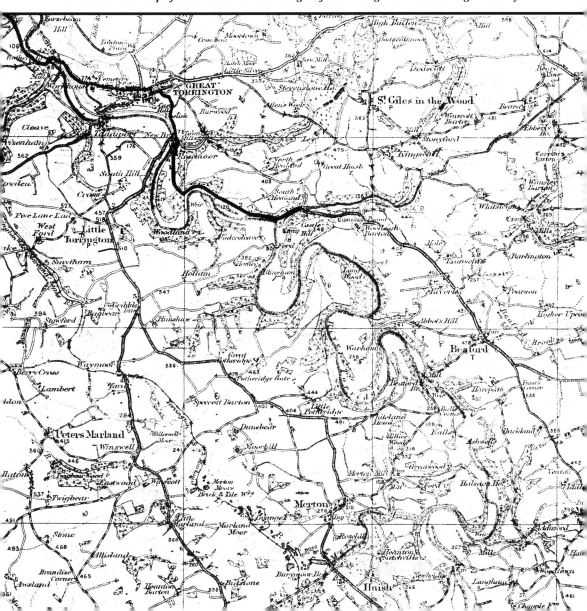

12. This view looks north, a short distance west of Torrington station, and has the railway's Marland (Torridge) Viaduct in the foreground. The Rothern road bridge is in the background. The postcard was sent on 2nd September 1905. (M.Dart coll.)

13. This undated scene looks north east at Watergate, where we see a loaded train in the loop waiting to proceed to Torrington. The locomotive is 0-6-0ST no.11 *Avonside*. It was built by the Avonside Engine Co in 1901 and was their works no.1428. (M.Dart coll.)

14.   Now we look at Yarde viaduct, as it was being rebuilt between 1921 and 1925. The work was carried out by Andersons and one of their works trains of side tipping wagons, is on the viaduct. The train is hauled by 0-4-0ST no.52 *Gyp* which was works no.761 built by Andrew Barclay in 1895. (M.Dart coll.)

15.   Here a train is heading from the ball clay works on the moors, to the cutting and drying sheds at Marland in the early 1960s. Hauling it is 4wDM *Forward*, which was a product of James Fowler. It was their works no. 3900012 and was built in 1947. (North Devon Shunter Group.)

16.   This scene looks south east at Marland works around 1900. On the left, is 0-4-0T no.3 *Peter* with a train from the mines. This locomotive was built in 1876 by Lewin. On the right waiting to work the train to Torrington, is 0-6-0ST no.1 *Mary*. This was works no.576 built by Black Hawthorn in 1880. *(North Devon Shunter Group)*

17.   This view, taken inside one of the drying sheds at Marland in the early 1960s, shows dried ball clay being loaded into two plank-wagons. *(North Devon Shunter Group)*

18.   *This photograph features the Lewin locomotive, no.3* Peter, *stopped with empty wagons near the ball clay mines. (M.Dart coll.)*

19.   *The railway possessed three Fletcher Jenning locomotives, which were rather heavy for the lightly laid track. The problem was overcome by removing the saddle tanks from the boiler tops and mounting them on flat trucks. The trucks were coupled to the locomotives and linked to them by hoses. This is* Jersey No.1 *on a train of loaded wagons at Marland Works, probably in the 1920s. Works no.129, this locomotive was built in 1873 and was rebuilt at Marland works in 1910. (North Devon Shunter Group)*

20.   A line up of diesel power at Marland works was recorded in the 1960s. From left to right the locomotives are: Advance *(JF 3930037/1949),* Forward *(JF 3900012/1947), no.2* Progress *(JF 4000001/1945),* Efficiency *(JF 3930048/1951) and no.1* Peter *(JF 22928/1940).* Progress *and* Peter *are both standard gauge, and are at the Bodmin & Wenford Railway. (North Devon Shunter Group)*

21.   During the 1900s some special excursion trains were operated to transport groups of visitors between Torrington and Marland works. This is a rare view of excursionists boarding one of these trains at Torrington. Boaters and caps appear in plenty and the ladies have umbrellas opened, to act as sunshades. Wooden planks have been placed across the wagons to act as rudimentary seats. (R.Handsford-Worth/R.Cook coll.)

PLYMOUTH & DARTMOOR RAILWAY -
LEE MOOR TRAMWAY

The well documented history of these two lines is quite complex so a book of this size could be devoted to each. A summary of the main facts is presented here. In 1785 Sir Thomas Tyrwhitt from Tor Royal at Princetown, commenced his plans to improve Dartmoor and in 1818 he promoted the Plymouth & Dartmoor Railway. The line was to supply lime to Dartmoor, as an aid to cultivation. It was also to bring peat from the moor, and granite from King Tor Quarry, to Plymouth. Preliminary Acts obtained were, for Crabtree to Princetown in 1819, an extension to Sutton Pool in 1820 and the Leigham tunnel diversion in 1821. The offices of the company were at the Rock Hotel at Yelverton. The major engineering work on the line was the Cann or Leigham Tunnel, which had a length of 600yd. There was 9ft 6in headroom in the tunnel, which was 109ft below ground at its deepest point. The line was laid to the gauge of 4ft 6in which became known as the 'Dartmoor' gauge. The line ran for 26 miles, from Cattedown to King Tor and was laid with cast iron rails of various types bolted on to stone sleeper blocks. In 1825 the line was extended to Sutton Harbour, with a branch to Laira (Martins) Wharf. The section from the quarries to Princetown opened in 1826. The Earl of Morley had worked a Blue Slatestone quarry in Cann Wood since at least 1664. As part of the agreement with him for permitting the line to pass through his land, another line was built from Crabtree to the south end of the Cann Quarry Canal at Marsh Mills. This opened between November 1829 and January 1830. In 1835 this line was extended to Plymbridge and parallel to the canal to access the quarry. A further branch line from Marsh Mills to Plympton opened in 1834. This was to carry china clay which had been brought by road from workings at Lee Moor. In 1847 the South Devon Railway was heading for Plymouth and in 1848 it purchased the Plympton branch of the PDR and closed it. This saved crossing the original line at Skew Bridge, Plympton. In 1851 the SDR purchased the PDR line to Sutton Harbour and laid a broad gauge rail on the formation. Similarly on 11th August 1883 a standard gauge line from Yelverton opened to Princetown, replacing the PDR line which had closed in 1878. The PDR was also involved in promoting lines to Turnchapel and Yealmpton. Next a line was built from the Cann Quarry branch at Plymbridge via Cann Wood Incline, to access the china clay works at Torycombe, from where another incline led to Lee Moor village. This line opened in 1854 but was poorly built and closed down on 20th March 1855. After rebuilding, the Lee Moor Tramway opened for traffic on 24th September 1858. A branch line opened from Lee Moor to Wotter, together with an extension from Lee Moor to Cholwichtown on 24th September 1858. The route was horse worked until 1899, when, after relaying the section above Cann Wood incline, steam locomotives were introduced between there and Torycombe. The total length of the line including branches was 9 ½ miles. In 1900 the section to Wotter closed with the Cholwichtown route following in 1933. Hardly any traffic passed over the line during the Second World War but, on 8th October 1945 the line re-opened to Torycombe. However, it closed completely on 31st December of that year, apart from the section between Marsh Mills and Mount Gould. A train of two or three wagons carried sand to Maddocks concrete works once a month, mainly to maintain the 'right of way' across the GWR main line at Laira Junction. This traffic ceased and the railway closed completely during October 1960. Until 9th April 1919 the line was owned by Martin Bros.Ltd; from when it became part of English China Clays, which from 12th October 1932, became English Clays Lovering Pochin & Co Ltd.

Further photographs appear in
Branch Lines Around Plymouth.

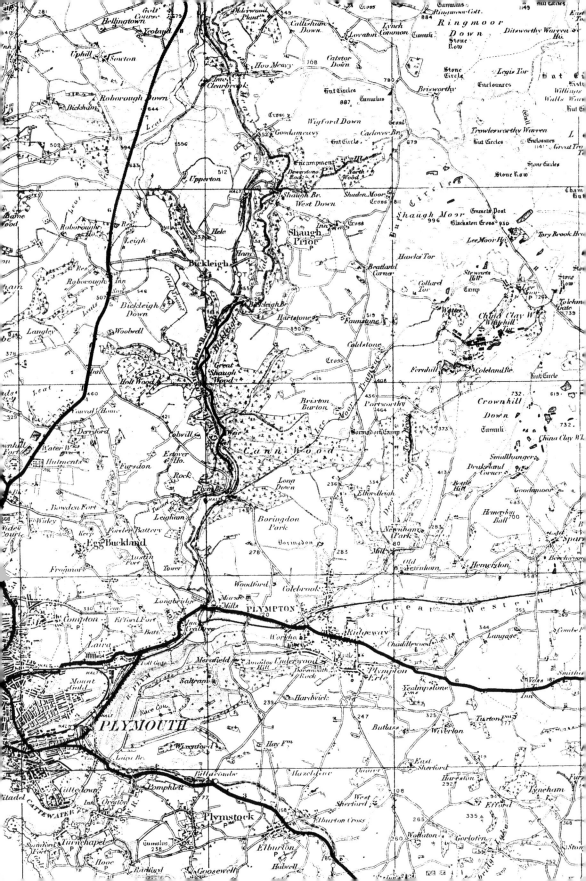

← ——— **XI.** *This 1 inch to 1 mile map dated 1919 shows the lines starting at Laira Wharf and running to Marsh Mills. The Plymouth & Dartmoor line curves off to the left and follows a sinuous route through Leigham Tunnel and heads off the map across Roborough Down. It is marked Old Tramway. The Lee Moor line runs north from Marsh Mills to Plym Bridge, where the Cann Quarry line runs on the east side of the GWR line to reach the quarry. The line to Lee Moor turns northeast towards the china clay works.*

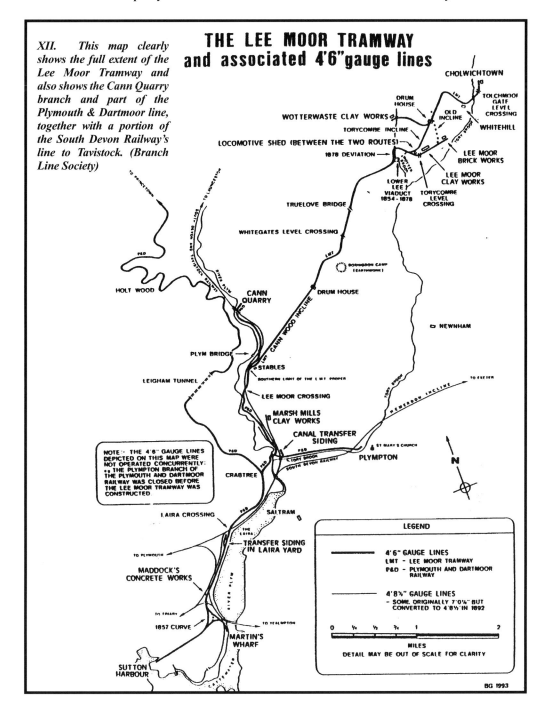

XII. *This map clearly shows the full extent of the Lee Moor Tramway and also shows the Cann Quarry branch and part of the Plymouth & Dartmoor line, together with a portion of the South Devon Railway's line to Tavistock. (Branch Line Society)*

THE LEE MOOR TRAMWAY
and associated 4'6"gauge lines

CHOLWICHTOWN

DRUM HOUSE

TOLCHMOOR GATE LEVEL CROSSING

WOTTERWASTE CLAY WORKS

OLD INCLINE

WHITEHILL

TORYCOMBE INCLINE

LOCOMOTIVE SHED (BETWEEN THE TWO ROUTES)

LEE MOOR BRICK WORKS

1878 DEVIATION

LOWER LEE VIADUCT 1854-1878

LEE MOOR CLAY WORKS

TORYCOMBE LEVEL CROSSING

TRUELOVE BRIDGE

WHITEGATES LEVEL CROSSING

DORNIGDON CAMP (EARTHWORK)

HOLT WOOD

CANN QUARRY

DRUM HOUSE

NEWNHAM

PLYM BRIDGE

STABLES

LEIGHAM TUNNEL

SOUTHERN LIMIT OF THE LMT PROPER

LEE MOOR CROSSING

TO EXETER

HEMERDON INCLINE

MARSH MILLS CLAY WORKS

CANAL TRANSFER SIDING

NOTE:- THE 4'6" GAUGE LINES DEPICTED ON THIS MAP WERE NOT OPERATED CONCURRENTLY: THE PLYMPTON BRANCH OF THE PLYMOUTH AND DARTMOOR RAILWAY WAS CLOSED BEFORE THE LEE MOOR TRAMWAY WAS CONSTRUCTED.

ST MARYS CHURCH

PLYMPTON

N

CRABTREE

SOUTH DEVON RAILWAY

LAIRA CROSSING

SALTRAM

TRANSFER SIDING IN LAIRA YARD

TO PLYMOUTH

MADDOCK'S CONCRETE WORKS

LEGEND

	4'6" GAUGE LINES
	LMT - LEE MOOR TRAMWAY
	P&D - PLYMOUTH AND DARTMOOR RAILWAY
	4'8½" GAUGE LINES
	- SOME ORIGINALLY 7'0¼" BUT CONVERTED TO 4'8½" IN 1892

TO FRIARY

1857 CURVE

MARTIN'S WHARF

TO YEALMPTON

SUTTON HARBOUR

0   ¼   ½   ¾   1   2

MILES
DETAIL MAY BE OUT OF SCALE FOR CLARITY

BG 1993

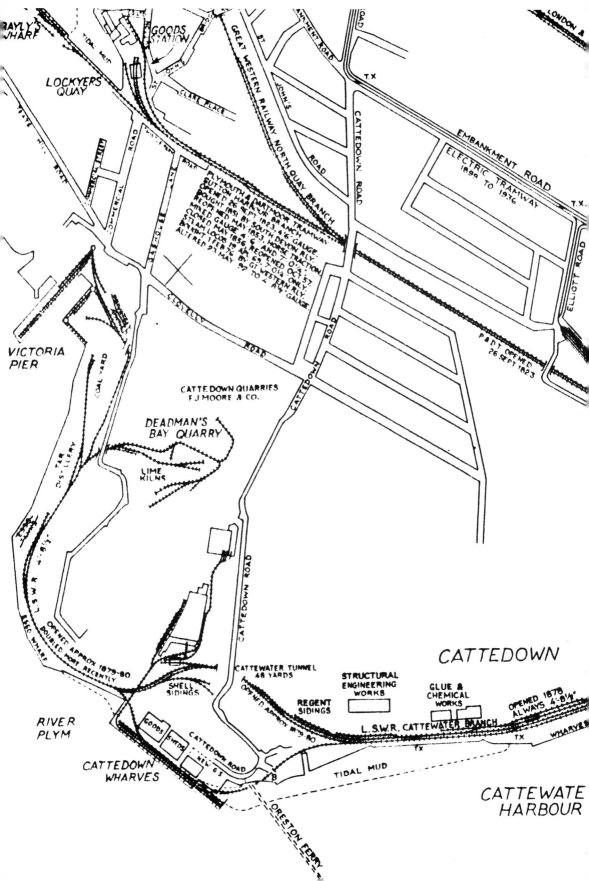

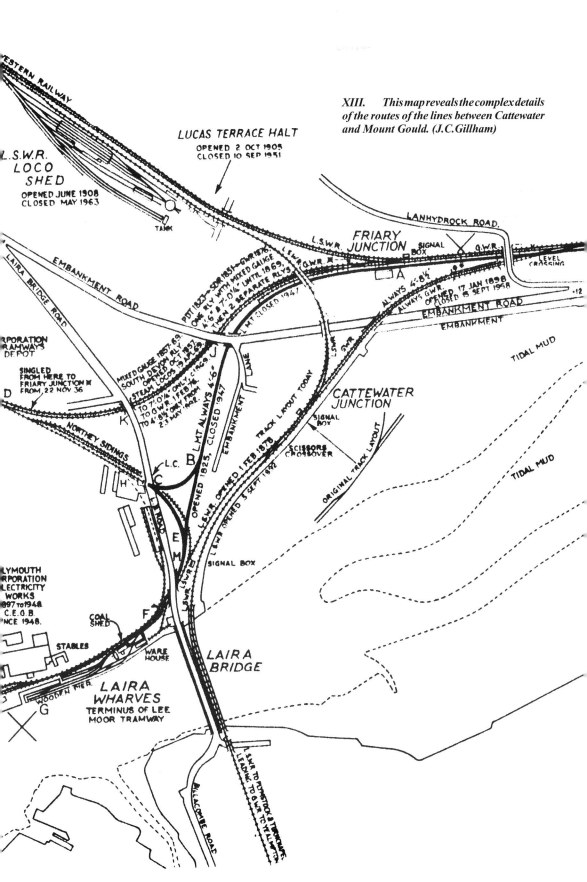

XIII.   This map reveals the complex details of the routes of the lines between Cattewater and Mount Gould. (J.C. Gillham)

LUCAS TERRACE HALT
OPENED 2 OCT 1905
CLOSED 10 SEP 1951

ESTERN RAILWAY

L.S.W.R.
LOCO
SHED
OPENED JUNE 1908
CLOSED MAY 1963

TANK

LANHYDROCK ROAD

FRIARY
JUNCTION

L.S.W.R.
G.W.R.
SIGNAL
BOX
A
G.W.R.
LEVEL
CROSSING

EMBANKMENT ROAD

LAIRA BRIDGE ROAD

PITT 1823—SDR 1851—GWR 1876
ONE RLY WITH MIXED GAUGE
4'6" & 7'0¼" UNTIL 1863,
THEN 2 SEPARATE RLYS
L.M.T. CLOSED 1947

L.S.W.R.
G.W.R.

ALWAYS 4'8½"
OPENED 17 JAN 1898
CLOSED 13 SEPT 1958

ALWAYS G.W.R.

EMBANKMENT ROAD
EMBANKMENT

+12

RPORATION
RAMWAYS
DEPOT

SINGLED
FROM HERE TO
FRIARY JUNCTION
FROM 22 NOV 36

D

MIXED GAUGE 1857-69,
SOUTH DEVON RLY
OPENED OCT 1857,
STEAM LOCOS 15 APL 58
TO 7'0¼" ONLY CIRCA 1869
TO G.W.R. 1 FEB 1876
TO 4'8½" ONLY FROM
23 MAY 1892.

K

L.C.

NORTHEY SIDINGS

H

C

B

L.M.T. ALWAYS 4'6"

L.S.W.R.

EMBANKMENT
LANE

L.M.T. OPENED 1825, CLOSED 1947

L.S.W.R. OPENED 1 FEB 1878

L.S.W.R. OPENED 3 SEPT 1892

TRACK LAYOUT TODAY

CATTEWATER
JUNCTION

SIGNAL
BOX

SCISSORS
CROSSOVER

ORIGINAL TRACK LAYOUT

TIDAL MUD

TIDAL MUD

E

M

SIGNAL BOX

L.M.S.D.

LYMOUTH
RPORATION
LECTRICITY
WORKS
897 to 1948.
C.E.G.B.
NCE 1948.

COAL
SHED

F

L.S.W.R.
G.W.R.

STABLES

WARE
HOUSE

LAIRA
BRIDGE

WOODEN PIER

G

LAIRA
WHARVES
TERMINUS OF LEE
MOOR TRAMWAY

L.S.W.R. TO PLYMSTOCK & TURNCHAPEL,
LEADING TO G.W.R. TO YEALMPTON

BILLACOMBE ROAD

22.   We start by looking northeast at the
terminus of the Lee Moor Tramway at Laira
Wharf in the late 1930s. Two empty wagons
on the left await return to Lee Moor, as Harry
Osborne leads a pair of horses towards the
stables, which are behind the photographer,
to the left. Harold Bray, the Shipping Captain,
stands by a line of wagons on the siding alongside
the River Plym. He is waiting for their loads of
lump clay to be transferred to a ship. The short
line in the foreground appears to be remnants
of a third siding. Part of the clay company office
and house are visible in the left background.
The mast of a ship protrudes above the loaded
wagons and the 'Iron' (Laira) bridge straddles
the river in the background. (A.Bray)

23.   The LMT headed northeast from
Laira Wharf and crossed the Southern
Railway's Cattewater branch line on the level
immediately before both lines passed under
Laira Bridge Road. We look south from the far
side of the bridge and see the company house
and office on the left of where the lines crossed.
The truncated remains of a spur off the SR line
are visible. This curved sharply into a cutting
to the right of the bridge, and latterly served
Pethicks yard. It had previously connected into
the GWR's Sutton Harbour branch. The base
of a signal box which protected the crossover,
is on the left. Road widening had occurred as is
evidenced by the newer section of the bridge at
the far end. This scene was recorded in 1955.
(R.Sambourne)

24.   Beyond the bridge the LMT swung away from the Cattewater branch and ran alongside the Sutton Harbour branch to Friary Junction from where it paralleled the SR main line. As it neared Mount Gould Junction, the LMT crossed the GWR no.2 spur from Cattewater Junction on the level; a train heading for Laira Wharf has just crossed it in about 1930. The four wagons appear to contain, in sequence, lump clay, bagged clay, bricks and sand, all of which were produced at Lee Moor. The driver is near the back of the first wagon. (Stephenson Locomotive Society)

25.   After the LMT passed Mount Gould Junction, it ran parallel with Laira marshalling yard, where there was a loop and a transfer siding. Two sets of empty wagons and one set of loaded wagons stand alongside an assortment of standard gauge rolling stock. Laira Junction signal box is on the right in this scene, from the 1920s. LMT wagons of two sizes are visible. (Stephenson Locomotive Society)

26.   After passing Laira Junction signal box, the LMT passed over the GWR main line at Laira Crossing, which a train is negotiating in the 1930s. The train consists of three empty wagons and one loaded with coal, on which the driver is perched holding the reins. The crossing was protected by signals on both lines, but the only gate was too short to completely block the GWR lines. The large GWR Laira locomotive sheds are in the background. (M.Dart coll.)

27.   Following Laira Crossing the line passed under Embankment Road and ran parallel with the River Plym for a distance before it swung inland, westwards. It headed towards and crossed the main road from Laira to Plympton at Crabtree. Before the crossing, a short siding which is shown in 1955 diverged to the right. A Western National Bristol double decked bus is passing over the level crossing. (R.Sambourne)

28.	The main line of the PDR headed east and north east and after crossing the Forder Valley Road, it ran in a cutting and entered Leigham (Cann) Tunnel. We view the south portal of the tunnel on 14th April 1993. It was firmly sealed up. (M.Dart)

29.	Now we return to follow the LMT which used the route of the PDR branch line to Cann Quarry. After crossing the road at Crabtree, the line turned north and paralleled the main road to Marsh Mills, where it diverged and crossed Forder Valley Road on the level. Next it curved to cross the River Plym by the bridge shown here in August 1928. The building beyond the bridge is the Toll / Weigh House. Some of the original weights used on the scales were located in the basement of this building in the 1950s. This bridge is still extant, but has a small bank at each end to prevent vehicular access. Beyond the bridge, remnants of LMT track remain buried. (R.S.Carpenter photographs)

30.	After passing Weighbridge Cottage the line swung left and followed the GWR Tavistock branch line. After passing Marsh Mills station, the LMT crossed the later siding to Coypool munitions depot, from where, after a fairly straight stretch, it crossed the Tavistock line at Lee Moor Crossing, south of Plym Bridge Halt. This scene from 1922 looks south at the crossing and shows the GWR signal box. The purpose of the siding off the LMT on the left, remains a mystery. It may have been a trap siding to catch any wagons that ran away down Cann Wood incline, or it may have been used to load timber during the First World War. It could have been used to transfer LMT steam locos onto GWR trolley wagons when they were being returned to Pecketts of Bristol for overhaul. (Stephenson Locomotive Society)

31.	Beyond Lee Moor Crossing, the PDR branch line to Cann Quarry diverged left and passed below the GWR Tavistock branch. It crossed a minor road and followed the bank of the canal to reach Cann Quarry. On 28th June 1959, we look south along the granite sleepers on the branch from a point halfway from the quarry to Plym Bridge. The trees on the left are overhanging the canal, which still contains a little water. (M.Dart)

32.   *After Lee Moor Crossing, the LMT passed its stables at the foot of Cann Wood incline. Near the foot of the incline, it crossed a timber trestle bridge, which is seen in the early 1920s. The bridge crossed the road from Plympton to Plym Bridge which was also crossed by the Tavistock line seen in the background. The bridge over the Cann Quarry branch is to the right of the bridge over the road. (F.H.C.Casbourn/Stephenson Locomotive Society)*

33.   *Six wagons of different sizes are descending Cann Wood incline in 1922 and have crossed the road trestle bridge and are approaching the incline foot. Rollers for cables are prominent. The double lines converge into single to cross the trestle bridge. The trackbed of the Cann Quarry branch is on the left. (F.H.C.Casbourn/Stephenson Locomotive Society)*

34.   After surmounting Cann Wood incline, the LMT crossed a short trestle bridge and passed through *Cann Wood drumhouse which is shown in the early 1920s. Just in front of the structure the cables descended into pits to the winding drums. Brake levers are just visible between the tracks inside the drumhouse. (F.H.C.Casbourn/Stephenson Locomotive Society)*

35.   From the drumhouse, the line ran north-east towards Lee Moor and crossed the Wotter to Plympton *road at Whitegates level crossing. The crossing was protected by manually worked signals and is viewed in May 1948 looking from the Lee Moor side. (R.Sambourne)*

36.   Around 500yd beyond Whitegates, the line entered a cutting in an area known locally as *The Ruts* near Truelove Farm. It passed under a minor road by Truelove bridge which we see looking towards Lee Moor in May 1948. A 66yd tunnel was originally proposed here. (R.Sambourne)

37.   From Truelove, the line ran through woods on the Wotter Curve which replaced a direct line that passed over the unstable Lower Lee Viaduct. The line entered the Lee Moor clay drying and brick making area at Torycombe. Before doing so it crossed this weighbridge which was recorded in May 1955. Remains of a gate which crossed the line lay in the bank. (M.Dart)

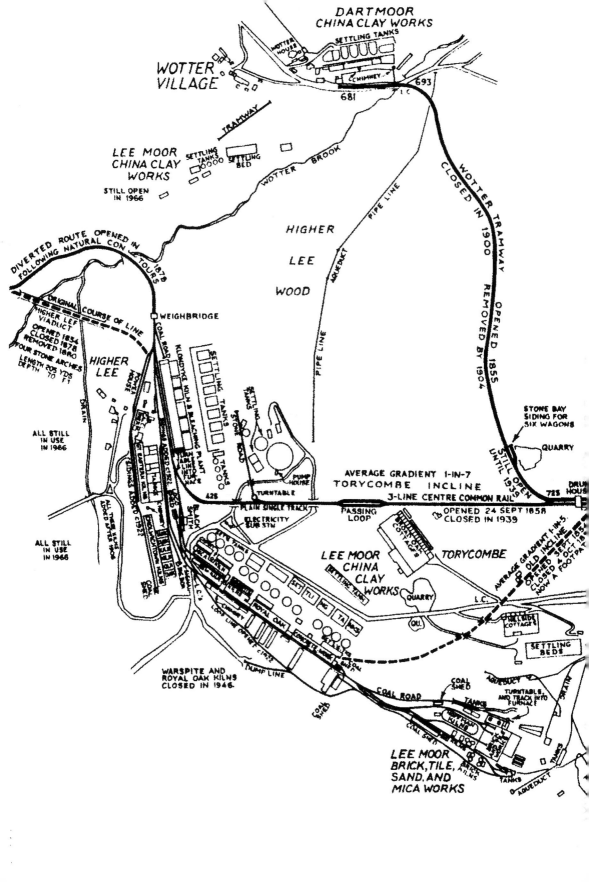

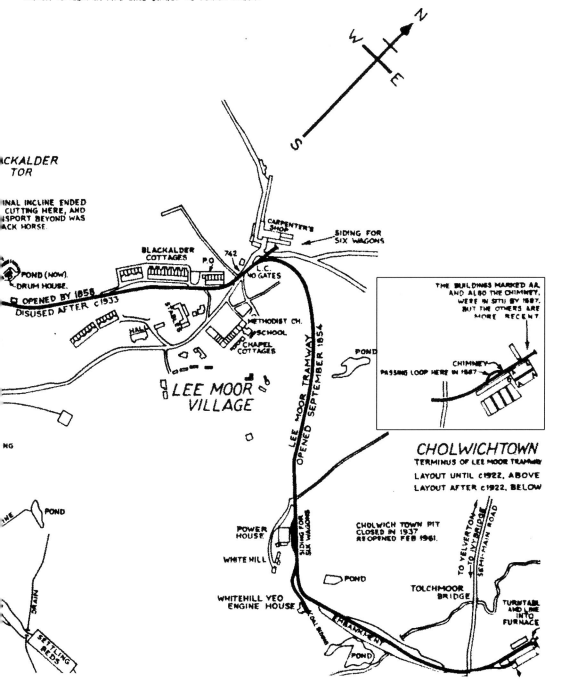

XIV.   This map shows detail of the lines of the Lee Moor Tramway east and north of Torycombe.
(J.C.Gillham)

OWNED 1866 TO 1900 BY WOTTER PORCELAIN CLAY WORKS CO.
OWNED 1900 TO 1910 BY SELLICK BROS LIMITED.
CLOSED 1910 TO 1921.
OWNED 1921 TO 1947 BY DARTMOOR CHINA CLAY CO.
OWNED 1947   BY ENGLISH CHINA CLAYS, LOVERING, POCHIN & CO. LTD

CHINA CLAY CARRIED 1855 TO 1900 BY HORSE TRAMWAY,
1900 TO 1910 BY SELLICK BROS BY STEAM LORRY TO CORNWOOD G.W.R. STATION (west of Ivybridge),
AND 1921 TO TODAY BY PIPE LINE DIRECT TO MARSH MILLS.

N
W E
S

BLACKALDER TOR

INAL INCLINE ENDED
CUTTING HERE, AND
SPORT BEYOND WAS
ACK HORSE.

POND (NOW).
DRUM HOUSE.
OPENED BY 1855
DISUSED AFTER c1933

BLACKALDER COTTAGES
P.O
742
L.C. NO GATES
CARPENTER'S SHOP
SIDING FOR SIX WAGONS

METHODIST CH.
SCHOOL
CHAPEL COTTAGES
HALL

POND

THE BUILDINGS MARKED AA, AND ALSO THE CHIMNEY, WERE IN SITU BY 1887, BUT THE OTHERS ARE MORE RECENT

CHIMNEY
PASSING LOOP HERE IN 1887

LEE MOOR VILLAGE

LEE MOOR TRAMWAY OPENED SEPTEMBER 1854

CHOLWICHTOWN
TERMINUS OF LEE MOOR TRAMWAY
LAYOUT UNTIL c1922, ABOVE
LAYOUT AFTER c1922, BELOW

NG

POND

POWER HOUSE

WHITE HILL

SIDING FOR SIX WAGONS

CHOLWICH TOWN PIT CLOSED IN 1937 REOPENED FEB 1961.

POND

TO YELVERTON TO IVYBRIDGE
SEPH-I-MAIN ROAD

TOLCHMOOR BRIDGE

TURNTABLE AND LINE INTO FURNACE

WHITEHILL YEO ENGINE HOUSE

COAL SIDING

TRAMWAY

SETTLING BEDS

MAIN

POND

38. This is a rare picture taken in the late 1930s in the works area at Torycombe. 0-4-0ST *Lee Moor No.2* **(Peckett 784/1899) is on a siding that served a china clay calciner. The line in the foreground ran northeast to the left to serve clay drying kilns and brick kilns. (Imerys Minerals)**

39.   This scene from around 1922 shows sidings that served *Cholwichtown* **kiln** at Torycombe. The siding, as was the usual practice, ran immediately below the outside wall of the clay storage area, which was called the linhay. (Imerys Minerals)

40.   After passing the calciner and three kilns, one line turned north and climbed Torycombe incline. Two other lines continued east and crossed the Plympton to Lee Moor road, on the level. A fitters shop and a locomotive shed were on the left side, before the level crossing. The locomotive shed is seen in May 1955 with part of the fitters shop on the right. The derelict sand tip of Wotter china clay pit is on the horizon. (M.Dart)

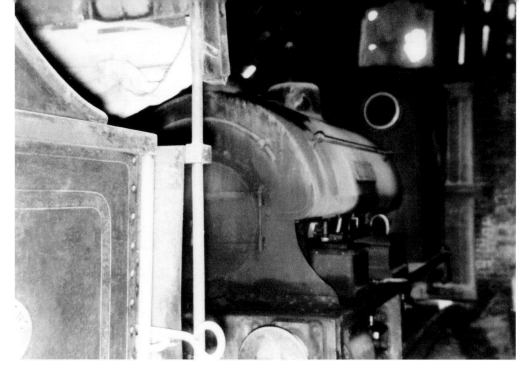

41.   We are inside the small locomotive shed at Torycombe on 19 th May 1953 with both of the engines present. The author stood on a bench beside *Lee Moor No.1* in order to record *Lee Moor No.2*, using a flash gun mounted on a box camera! (M.Dart)

42.   Torycombe level crossing was protected by signals, worked from a signal box seen in May 1955, with a rake of derelict wagons alongside it. An equally derelict signal is visible over the top of the wagons. A structure just visible above the top left of the wagons on Crownhill Down is Kellys Winder. This housed a stationary steam engine for a cable worked sand tip incline in the Torycombe valley. (M.Dart)

43.	This view of the disused Torycombe level crossing in 1947 shows the line that crossed the road to serve brick kilns and clay kilns. The building on the right housed a clay mill. Another line crossed the road and ran between kilns on the left. The derelict signal is prominent and Kellys Winder is on Crownhill Down. (K.Brown)

44.	Here we see *Lee Moor No.1* (Peckett 783/1899) on Torycombe level crossing in the 1920s with clay kilns behind the engine. The road curves past the engine to climb the hill to Lee Moor village. (F.H.C.Casbourn/ Stephenson Locomotive Society)

45.		This view which dates from around 1922 looks west from the back end of Lee Moor brick works at Torycombe. Sidings with a connecting spur are visible, with bee-hive and rectangular brick kilns between them. Mid-picture, in the background, is the large Hoffmann brick kiln. Clay kilns with their chimneys are in the distance. Two wagons in the left foreground are loaded with sand from Torycombe Valley sand tip. (Imerys Minerals)

46.		The original route of the tramway from Torycombe to Lee Moor diverged halfway from the level crossing to the brickworks and ascended the Old Torycombe incline. There was negative superelevation on a curve at the bottom of this incline and it fell out of use after a few months. Part of the way up this incline the route crossed the road to Lee Moor village. Immediately before crossing the road, the line passed through a spoil tip from a quarry. After the cutting had been dug out, stone walls were built on each side to stabilise the sides. We look down through the cutting to the Torycombe Valley on 14th April 1993. (M.Dart)

47.   Now we return to the west of Torycombe level crossing and look at the line to Lee Moor village, in 1922, as it started to ascend the New Torycombe incline. Note the rollers to carry the haulage cable at the side of the line by the bank. (F.H.C.Casbourn/Stephenson Locomotive Society)

48.   This view from 1930 looks at the drumhouse at the top of the New Torycombe incline. Steps inside the circular building to the right of the drumhouse gave access to the winding drum. On the far right is the incline lookout man's tower. It contained a bell and he had an unrestricted view down the incline from the small window. The line on the right is at the top of the incline and has a wooden chock in place. A wagon is outside the back of the drumhouse. Rails on the line on the left, which is from Wotter kilns, are laid on stone blocks. (Stephenson Locomotive Society)

49.　　Torycombe incline was self-acting and traffic coming up was counterbalanced by a pair of wagons which were filled with water for the descent. Two different pairs of wagons had been used and the later pair is seen near the drumhouse in the 1930s. (Stephenson Locomotive Society)

50.　　This view from May 1955 looks northwest along the formation of the line to Wotter clay kilns. Two lines of stone block sleepers are to be seen, with the sand tips from Wotter clay pit in the mid-distance. The route is passing through First Style. (M.Dart)

51.   From Torycombe incline drumhouse, the line ran towards and entered Lee Moor village. After skirting several rows of houses, the track crossed the road at the top of the hill and passed through the works area, which we see, in the early 1900s. Wagons of coal are being unloaded in front of the carpenters and wheelrights shops and stores. Piles of timber and wheels for horse drawn wagons can be seen on the right, as a horse standing near the buildings surveys the scene. (M.Dart coll.)

52.   From Lee Moor village, the line ran east across the moor and passed Lee Moor Old power station which was served by a siding. This view from May 1955 shows the main route climbing past the building on the left, with the formation of the siding running in the gulley beside the building and passing under the bridge, which gave access to it. This building is extant. The main route curved to the left and passed the steam powered winder for Whitehill Yeo sand tip incline. The chimney of the winder is in the left distance. (M.Dart)

53.   This is the view obtained of Whitehill Yeo incline winder, as the author surmounted the top of the incline in May 1955. The haulage cable passed through the opening in the wall. A siding that was used to deliver coal served the winder and joined the main route to the right of the photo. The main route is visible running on a bank flanked by posts behind the winder. (M.Dart)

54.   Shortly after passing the junction of the siding from the winder, the line crossed the road from Lee Moor to Cornwood at Tolchmoor Gate and approached the terminus at Cholwichtown kilns. This scene of barren dereliction at the kilns was recorded on 11 th May 1961. Cholwichtown is locally pronounced as Challistun. (R.Sambourne)

REDLAKE RAILWAY

The China Clay Corporation operated clay works in a remote area of Dartmoor around Redlake and Leftlake north east of Ivybridge on Dartmoor. To carry workmen, sand, coal and other supplies to the works, a seven mile long 3ft gauge railway was laid from the drying kiln at Cantrell, adjacent to the GWR main line, across the moor to the clay works, which was 600ft above sea level. A cable-worked incline climbed from Cantrell to the moor, from where locomotives were used. During construction of the railway, a temporary 2ft gauge line was used. The route opened in September 1911 and was operated by the Ivybridge China Clay Co Ltd from 1921. The line closed when the clay works shut in 1932 and was dismantled in 1933.

XV.   The route followed by the Redlake Railway has been drawn in on this OS map from 1956. The southernmost section of the line is not shown. Part of the much earlier 5ft gauge Zeal Tor Tramway is also shown. (OS/M.Dart)

Further photographs appear in **Newton Abbot to Plymouth**.

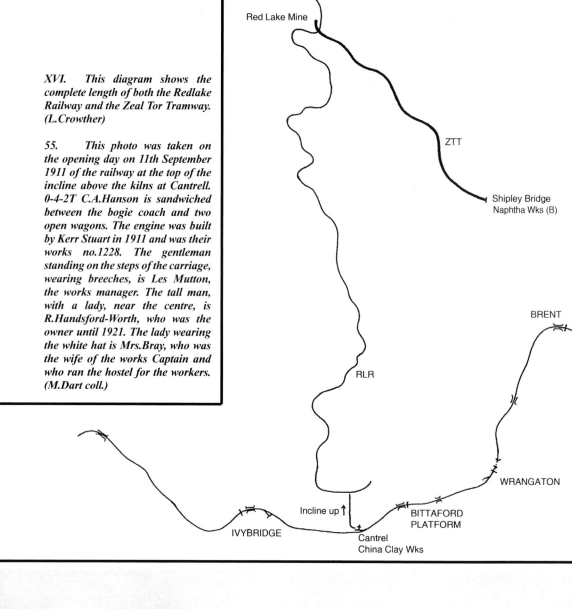

XVI. This diagram shows the complete length of both the Redlake Railway and the Zeal Tor Tramway. (L.Crowther)

55. This photo was taken on the opening day on 11th September 1911 of the railway at the top of the incline above the kilns at Cantrell. 0-4-2T C.A.Hanson is sandwiched between the bogie coach and two open wagons. The engine was built by Kerr Stuart in 1911 and was their works no.1228. The gentleman standing on the steps of the carriage, wearing breeches, is Les Mutton, the works manager. The tall man, with a lady, near the centre, is R.Handsford-Worth, who was the owner until 1921. The lady wearing the white hat is Mrs.Bray, who was the wife of the works Captain and who ran the hostel for the workers. (M.Dart coll.)

Red Lake Mine

ZTT

Shipley Bridge
Naphtha Wks (B)

BRENT

RLR

WRANGATON

Incline up ↑

BITTAFORD
PLATFORM

IVYBRIDGE

Cantrel
China Clay Wks

56.   Carriage no.1 is near the top of the incline at Cantrell in 1933. (F.H.C.Casbourn/ Stephenson Locomotive Society)

57.   As the line climbed over the moor, rotting wooden sleepers and bolts remained in place around 1950. They were lying amongst rough stone ballast that was laid after closure to convert the trackbed into a rough road. (H.S.A.Fox)

58. _Running through such high and exposed areas, the line experienced severe winters, with snowstorms such as depicted here on an unknown date, but soon after the loco arrived in 1928. It was a four wheeled, vertical boilered locomotive named Lady Mallaby-Deeley which was works no.111 of Atkinson & Walker, built in 1928. The driver is Harry Fox whilst the gentleman on the ground is the works captain, George Bray. Note the large cast nameplate on the side of the locomotive and the name of the builder on the top of the front of the cab. When the line closed in 1933, this engine worked the demolition train. (Locomotive & General Railway Photographs)_

59. _The derelict locomotive shed is seen about 1950. It was on a short spur off the main route, near the top of the incline at Cantrell. (H.S.A.Fox)_

SHAUGH IRON MINE TRAMWAY
SHAUGH PRIOR

60. _This is one of the few views that have been discovered to include this obscure tramway. We look south from a position above the east bank of the River Plym, south of Shaugh Bridge. Rails and sleepers mark the course of the tramway as it runs along the east bank of the river, down Bickleigh Vale. (M.Dart coll.)_

The Shaugh Iron Mine was situated a short distance south of Shaugh Bridge several hundred yards east of the river, and a tramway, thought to be of 2ft gauge, exited the mine via the adit and ran towards the river. It turned south and followed the bank and ended near a bridge across the river, from where a road led to Bickleigh station. At Bickleigh, a small goods shed and siding at the south end of the station opened for traffic on 1st February 1860 and ore from the mine was transhipped there. During the boring of Shaugh (Lee Beer) Tunnel, a siding was provided for use by engineers, 21 chains south of the portal. This siding appears to have been removed when the line opened for traffic, but was relaid and reopened on 1st August 1870 to load low grade iron ore produced at a mine below Shaugh Bridge on the east side of the river. So this indicates that the mine used this siding from that date, which probably ended the use of the tramway. The ore was taken to Plymouth for shipment to South Wales for smelting. It is recorded that the mines output between 1870 and 1874 was 4670 tons. The siding was out of use and was removed to enable the construction of Shaugh Bridge Platform which opened to passengers on 19th October 1907.

XVII. The route of the tramway has been drawn on this OS map of 1907. The line ran south from Squares Iron Mine towards the river, east of Thrill Wood. (OS/M.Dart)

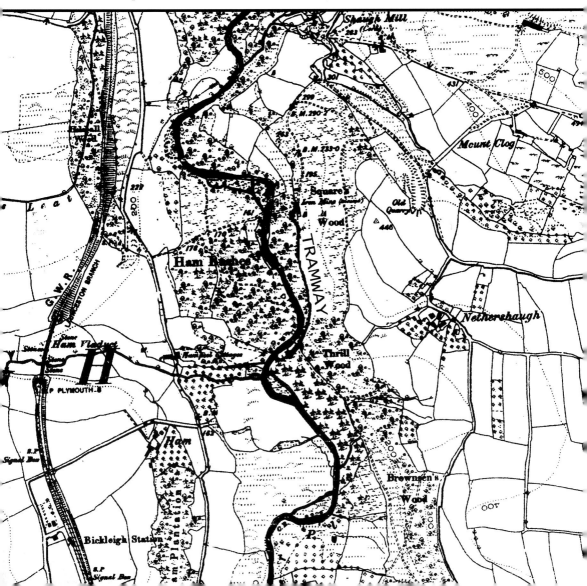

SIDMOUTH HARBOUR RAILWAY

In 1836, an Act was passed enabling the Sidmouth Harbour Co to build a jetty at Chit Rocks to form a harbour. It was to be constructed using large blocks of stone from a quarry one and three quarter miles to the east at Hook Ebb. To transport the stone a 3ft 6in gauge 'woodway' was built along the esplanade, which crossed a viaduct over the River Sid, before entering a one third of a mile long tunnel through Salcombe Hill cliff. Supports for the viaduct were tree trunks with pointed ends reinforced with metal, which were driven into the ground. The west portal of the tunnel had a clearance of around 6ft. A locomotive was purchased and arrived by sea at Hook Ebb, but its height precluded it passing through the tunnel. So the locomotive was hauled by packs of horses over steep and winding paths to Sidmouth, where it was put to work hauling a carriage along the length of the esplanade, providing trips. The locomotive was said to be of 3ft 8in gauge and was almost certainly built by the Neath Abbey Iron Works and was probably named **Hawk**. During 1837 the company ran out of funds and abandoned the project. By 1838 the locomotive had been disposed of, the viaduct had been demolished by sawing through the supports and the tunnel portals had been blocked.

61.   We are at the north end of the promenade at Sidmouth on a very stormy 31st January 1995. We look across where a viaduct once carried the line over the River Sid and see the south portal of the tunnel which passed through Salcombe Hill cliff. This portal had been sealed for a great many years, but ferocious seas and heavy rain had washed part of the cliff away, to expose the long-lost tunnel. (M.Dart)

————➤   *The Westleigh Stone & Lime Co Ltd worked extensive limestone quarries north of Westleigh village. The Bristol & Exeter Railway laid a 3ft gauge line in 1873 from the quarries to connect with their main line three quarters of a mile away at Burlescombe. In 1898 the Quarry Company took over the line and relaid it to standard gauge but retained an internal 3ft gauge system. Road transport took over from 1950 and all remaining rails were removed. The quarry became part of the ECC Group.*

————➤ *XVIII. This section of an OS map from 1906 shows the standard gauge branch line leading to the works with narrow gauge lines running to the quarry.*

62.   This interesting scene at the quarry dates from 1898 or early 1899. One of the Bristol & Exeter Railway 3ft gauge 0-4-0 well tanks is on the trestle hauling a train of assorted side tipping wagons. This would be one of either GWR nos.1381 or 1382. The numberplate was carried on the back plate of the cab. These engines were BER nos. 111 and 112 and were built in 1873 and in 1875. They were sold to the Bute Works Supply Co in March 1899. The locomotive on the lower standard gauge line is Manning Wardle 0-6-0ST Cantreff which was their works no. 1235 of 1893. It was obtained from Cardiff Corporation Water Works after 2nd August 1898 and went to Pecketts in 1926 in part exchange for a new locomotive. The workers appear to be interested in the photographer. (Imerys Minerals) ————➤

WESTLEIGH QUARRY
BURLESCOMBE

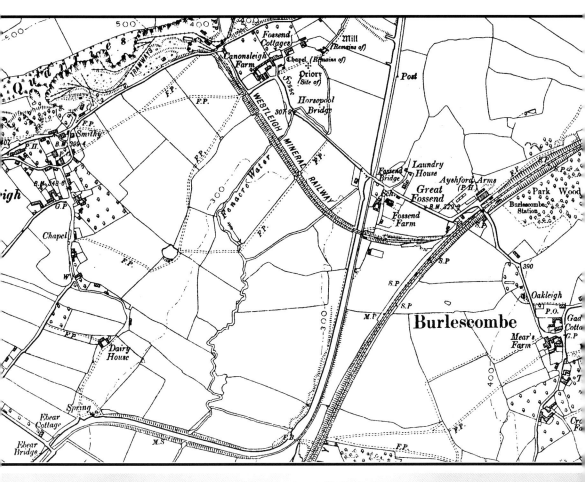

2. Military

EFFORD FORT
PLYMOUTH

This fort was part of the early defences of Plymouth. During the Second World War the fort was used as an ammunition store and a 2ft gauge manually worked tramway was laid, linking the entrance yard with storage areas. After hostilities ceased, the system fell out of use and the fort is now used as winter quarters for fairground operators, but many of the rails remain.

XIX. *This is a diagrammatic representation of the part of the layout of the fort, showing the tramway. (M.Dart/S.Parkinson)*

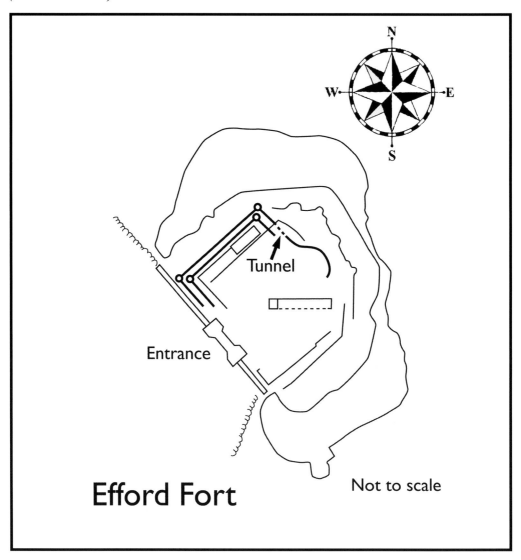

63.   A line ran from the outside yard, past the inner wall, to a point where two turntables on it gave access to lines that ran along each side of a compound. This is the line which continued along the inside of the outer wall of the fort and passed a set of Casemates. Latterly these had formed part of the storage complex and were recorded on 7th April 2004. (M.Dart)

64.   Both lines ran to the end of the compound, but the inner one passed over another turntable from where a line climbed through a tunnel that passed through ground floor structures to reach an inner yard, where it served further stores on the next storey up. We are two thirds of the way through the tunnel and see the line emerging as it climbed towards the next level. The outer wall, which has the remains of battlements at the top, is beyond the tunnel. Doors on the left once accessed the interior, but the hooks on the right hand wall are a later addition. (M.Dart)

FROWARD POINT
KINGSWEAR

During the Second World War defences were constructed under the cliffs here and a 2ft gauge tramway was laid to carry ammunition from storage bunkers down to the gun emplacements. After the war had ended, the defences fell out of use and were removed, but the tramway rails remain.

65. *This photograph was taken on 5th September 1998 from a point roughly two thirds of the way down the double track incline. The gradient has eased at this point as the rails approach the site of the emplacements on which the gun batteries were mounted. These face directly out over the mouth of the River Dart. Steps lead from the ground up to where the batteries were mounted. There were other fortifications around to the right. (M.Dart)*

66.   On the same day we turn and climb a little and look up the top section of the incline to storage buildings. (M.Dart)

67.   Again on the same date we have reached the incline top, where the base plate of a winch remained. The door of one of the empty storage buildings was open. Many more such buildings were dotted around in the woods above here. (M.Dart)

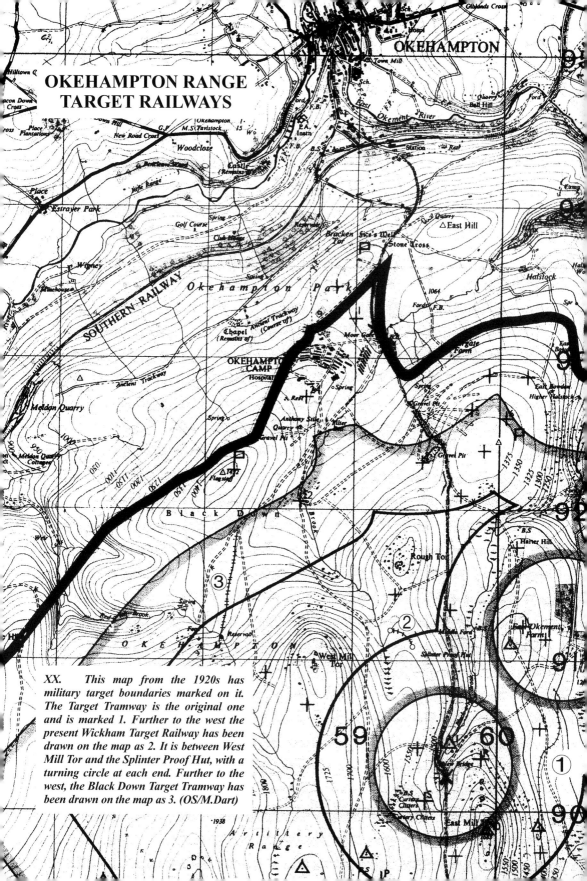

OKEHAMPTON RANGE
TARGET RAILWAYS

XX. This map from the 1920s has military target boundaries marked on it. The Target Tramway is the original one and is marked 1. Further to the west the present Wickham Target Railway has been drawn on the map as 2. It is between West Mill Tor and the Splinter Proof Hut, with a turning circle at each end. Further to the west, the Black Down Target Tramway has been drawn on the map as 3. (OS/M.Dart)

68. This view looks north west from the bottom of the east side of East Mill Tor on 14th July 2005. A section of the track of the original Target Tramway remains where the line crossed a brook immediately before it crossed the road, which now encircles the western section of the ranges. Behind the photographer many more rails remained buried under soil as the line climbed the side of East Mill Tor in a low cutting. Beyond the road the line curved in a shallow cutting where the tops of two people walking the route can be discerned. (M.Dart)

The original line, known as the Target Tramway, was laid during the Boer War. The 18in gauge track ran from the east side of East Mill Tor down the side of the moor to the valley of the East Okement river, which it crossed by a lightly built bridge. A branch off this line ran towards East Okement Farm. Targets mounted on trolleys gravitated down the line which crossed the road that was constructed in 1901. Targets were hauled back by horses. A 2ft 6in gauge tramway was laid around the time of the Second World War, east of West Mill Tor, but around 1942 this was lifted and relaid on an alignment south east of the original formation. This track was reconditioned in 2004 and is known as H1 or the Wickham Target Railway. Another 2ft gauge line called the Black Down Tramway dated from 1942. This was a winch-worked line that ran for about one mile and descended the side of Black Down. It approached the upper stretches of the Red-a-Ven Brook which it ran alongside to a terminal point. No rails are extant, but pulleys, parts of a winch and the walls of the engine house remain. Three target tramways have existed at Willsworthy Range, northeast of the twin villages of Mary and Peter Tavy. Rails are only present on the easternmost tramway near Reddaford Farm enclosure and date from around 1911.

69. This is the north west end of the later Wickham Target Tramway on 20th October 2001. We see points with their lever, which gave access to the balloon loop at that end. The line climbed away, in what at that time was a waterlogged cutting. Beyond the summit, the line gradually descended and curved to reach the balloon loop at the south eastern end. Since this picture was taken, the line has been reconditioned by the MOD. This entailed blowing up sections of the line including that shown in the cutting, as live ordnance was discovered under the trackbed. Most of the track has been relaid and reballasted. (M.Dart)

70.   *A spur off the north west balloon loop ran to a two line shed where the two Wickham trolleys were housed when not in use. With its closed entrance doors in deep shadow, the structure was recorded on 20th October 2001. This shed has since been rebuilt by the MOD. (M.Dart)*

71.   *During the visit on 14th July 2005 the shed was opened, and the reconditioned target towing trolley was manually propelled outside for photography. This trolley had been reclaimed by the MOD from the Museum of Dartmoor Life at Okehampton where it had been on loan for several years, but had not been displayed. It was built by Wickhams in 1943 as no.3284. It carried the MOD no.767138 and had been named Captain. The extended side and end frames are used to mount a target. The second Wickham that was at the site is at present displayed at the Leighton Buzzard Railway. (M.Dart)*

RNAD ERNESETTLE
PLYMOUTH

Between 1922 and 1926 extensive storage facilities for munitions were constructed on the east bank of the River Tamar. Surface buildings and large underground storage areas were linked to exchange sidings with standard gauge lines and to a jetty by a network of 2ft 6in gauge lines. Road transport replaced the narrow gauge railway in 1980 and the track was removed that year. Internal lines of 18in gauge served the nearby depot at Bullpoint from the early 1920s until 1958, but no photos of that system have been located.

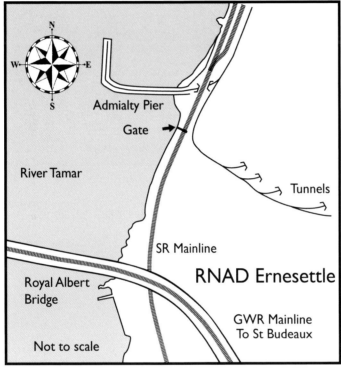

Further photos appear in Newton Abbot to Plymouth

XXI.   Route of the line from the Admiralty pier to the exchange sidings and the curve to the storage tunnels. (M.Dart/S.Parkinson)

72.   Diesel no.5 (HE 2244/ 1941) hauls what appears to be a loaded train off the Admiralty pier towards the exchange sidings from where a line climbed, curved and threw off spurs to the storage tunnels. The author was with the photographer when this scene was recorded on 26th May 1956. Although we were standing outside the perimeter gate, the photographer was challenged and reprimanded by the security guard on duty. (M.Daly)

3. Main Line Owned

LYNTON & BARNSTAPLE RAILWAY

As a volume which is almost completely devoted to this line has been published by Middleton Press, I have only included a representative selection of views of the line which were not in that book. This 19 mile line of 1ft 11 ½ in gauge from Barnstaple Town to Lynton was opened on 18th May 1898. The company was absorbed into the Southern Railway on 1st January 1923 and closed completely on 29th September 1935. The equipment was auctioned in November of the same year and the track was removed completely by the summer of 1937.

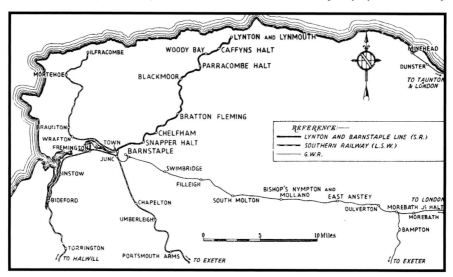

XXII. The route of the line in the 1920s. (Railway Magazine)

73.   *We look south at Barnstaple Town station on an unknown date as 2-6-2T* Lew *is waiting in the bay platform with a short train for Lynton. The LSWR line to Ilfracombe is on the right. The stationmaster, staffs of both of the railways, and a dog watch the photographer. (M.Dart coll.)*

74.   This is a view of the locomotive and carriage sheds at Pilton Yard, which was a short distance along the line from Barnstaple Town. The locomotive is either *Yeo* or *Exe* and the photo appears to have been taken in the early 1920s. (Photomatic/Rail Archive Stephenson)

Further photographs of this line may be found in Branch Line to Lynton.

---

75.   We look east in the early 1900s to Chelfham viaduct with the station situated immediately beyond it. This viaduct is a listed structure and has been completely restored ready to receive rails again at some future date. (Lynton Station)

76.   Now we have a photograph taken in the period when the SR owned the line. Looking east we see *2-6-2T no.188 Lew* which has stopped at *Bratton Fleming station* with a train bound for *Barnstaple Town.* There is a short siding at the far end on the left. (Pamlin Prints)

77.   We are looking east again, but are now at Blackmoor Gate in 1900. A carriage is on the short siding at the west end of the station. The bridge in the distance has been filled in and the area now forms the approach and parking space for the Old Station House Inn that occupies the original building. (Lynton & Barnstaple Railway)

78.   This view looks east at Lynton in the early 1900s. 2-6-2T Lew is waiting to depart with a mixed train for Barnstaple Town. The station building and goods shed are still extant. (Lynton Station)

79.   Yeo, Exe, Taw and Lew were all 2-6-2Ts but the odd man out was 2-4-2T Lyn. We have a close up of this latter locomotive waiting to depart from Lynton on a Barnstaple Town train in the early 1920s. The small locomotive shed can be seen in the left background. (Photomatic/Rail Archive Stephenson)

4. TOURIST

BICTON WOODLAND RAILWAY
BUDLEIGH SALTERTON

A line around 1000yd in length to a gauge of 18in was laid in Bicton Gardens and opened on 6 April 1963. Use of the line gradually declined, but during 2000 it was re-equiped and was brought into regular use.

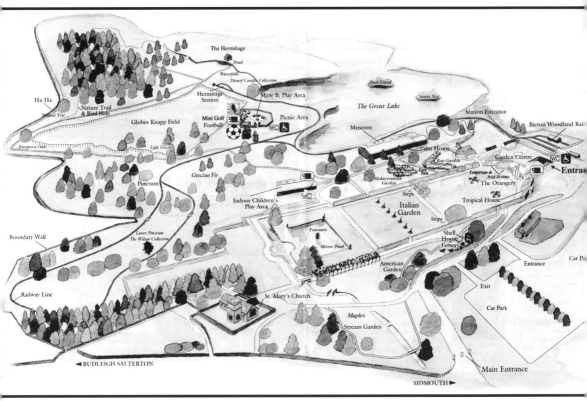

(left) **XXIII. This schematic drawing shows the layout of the gardens with the railway running from the centre right. (Bicton Park)**

(lower left) **80. This is a general view of Bicton station taken on 4th January 2007. The water tank and stores are on the left, next to the locomotive and carriage shed. Stabled in the yard with a spare set of carriages is 4wDM** *Clinton* **(HE 2290/1941). At the head of the train in the station is steam-outline 0-4-0DH** *Sir Walter Raleigh***, which was built by Alan Keef, as works no.61 in 2000. (M.Dart)**

(top) **81. Here is a close up view of** *Sir Walter Raleigh* **at the head of its train. It is underneath the canopy at Bicton station on the same date. Bicton is on the left on the spare set of stock. (M.Dart)**

82. After running around a long horseshoe loop through woodland, the train returned to a triangular junction where it swung away and climbed north east to reach Hermitage station. In this photograph, taken on the same day, *Sir Walter Raleigh* **has run around the train and is awaiting departure from Hermitage. (M.Dart)**

C. BURGES
CHRISTOW STATION

This private system on the site of Christow station is known as the Exeter & Teign Valley Railway. It opened around mid 1993 and contains lines of standard, 2ft and 18in gauge.

83. **A wide assortment of narrow gauge wagons is evident at Christow during a visit by members of Plymouth Railway Circle on 17th June 2000. In the background is standard gauge 0-4-0DM** *Perseus.* **A narrow gauge diesel locomotive has been acquired since this visit. The hoppers in the background are remnants of the nearby quarry workings that provided a source of freight traffic for the line. (M.Dart)**

84. **During the same visit, manually powered rides were available in this carriage called** *Jenny Wren.* **(M.Dart)**

DEVON RAILWAY CENTRE
CADELEIGH STATION

This small railway museum opened in 1997 and is undergoing further development. A passenger-carrying 2ft gauge line around 800yd in length was opened and has been followed by a passenger-carrying miniature line of similar length. There are also standard gauge exhibits and the original station buildings.

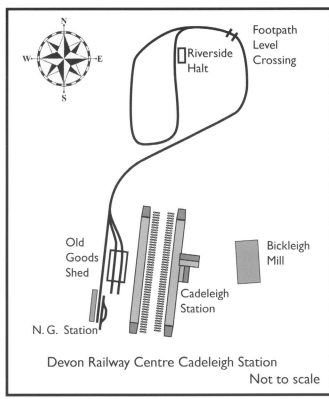

Devon Railway Centre Cadeleigh Station

Not to scale

XXIV. This drawing shows the route the line follows on the west side of the trackbed of the standard gauge route. (M.Dart/S.Parkinson)

85.   A train hauled by 0-4-0ST Pixie on 9th December 2006 has completed circuits of the two horseshoe loops and has arrived back at the station and the driver chats to passengers who have detrained. The locomotive will uncouple, take water and run around the train, ready for the next departure. The locomotive dates from 1922 and is Kerr Stuart works no.4260. It was on loan from the Leighton Buzzard Railway. The old goods shed in the background serves as a locomotive shed and repair shop. The original station building is seen on the right, with standard gauge carriages in the platform. These carriages are home to several very interesting model railway layouts. The miniature railway runs to the left of the fence behind the narrow gauge platform. (M.Dart)

86.   Halfway around the easternmost of the horseshoe loops there is Riverside Halt. The very basic station is viewed from a carriage as the train slowly passed on 9th December 2006. Trains do not stop there out of season. (M.Dart)

87.   Several 2ft gauge diesel locomotives are on display near the narrow gauge station. One was a Planet, one a Ruston & Hornsby with one unidentified specimen. A standard gauge Baguley diesel is on the right. (M.Dart)

88. *Several diesel locomotives were noted awaiting restoration behind the old goods shed during the 9th December visit. Permission was obtained to record these whilst the narrow gauge train stopped at the terminus. At the east end, surrounded by a mass of muddy ground, was this unidentifiable 4w Motor Rail (Simplex) machine. (M.Dart)*

EXMOOR STEAM RAILWAY
BRATTON FLEMING

Construction and overhaul of narrow gauge steam locomotives are carried out by June and Trevor Stirland, assisted by their daughter Julie and son Tony at Cape of Good Hope Farm. During the 1990s passengers were carried on a 15 inch gauge line, which extended for about one mile. In the mid 1990s the line was relaid to the gauge of 12¼ inches. However passenger carrying operations ceased in 2003 and the site closed to the public.

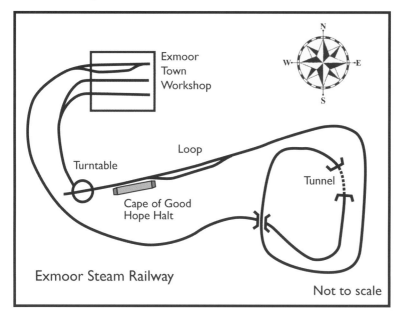

XXV. This diagram shows the approximate route of the line. (M.Dart/S.Parkinson)

89. The platform at Exmoor Town station is under cover and adjoins the workshops which are behind the photographer. On 23rd February 2007 0-4-2T (works no.191) Lorna Doone *is at the platform on a short rake of carriages. Partly hidden on the line behind is 0-4-2T* Denzil *which is on another train. (M.Dart)*

90.　　Seen in around 2001, 2-8-0T *Yeo Valley* (works no.190) is at Exmoor Town. It is in the loop with a spare set of carriages. (M.Dart coll.)

91.　　During a pre-arranged visit to the site on 23rd February 2007 an amazing nine locomotives were in various states of assembly in the Erecting Shop. One of these was this 7¼ inch gauge 0-4-2T. A locomotive of the same type is in the right background and the frames of a different type of locomotive are to the left. (M.Dart)

92.	Three 2ft gauge ex-South African Railways 2-6-2 + 2-6-2T Beyer-Garratt locomotives are in the works yard awaiting restoration. During the visit on 23rd February 2007, no.115 stands in front of partly obscured no.130. *(M.Dart)*

93.	Having ridden the train from Exmoor Town to Cape of Good Hope Halt, one alighted whilst the run-round manoeuvre was carried out. On 29th August 1999, *Denzil* is backing on to carriages at the platform, which was situated very awkwardly for photography. A small tender is attached to the locomotive. This was provided to carry air braking equipment which comprised an air tank, a compressor and valves. *(M.Dart)*

LYNBARN LIGHT RAILWAY
NEAR CLOVELLY

This 2ft gauge line at Milky Way Farm Park was 750yd in length. It opened on 10th May 1994 and was operated by a group who proposed to plough any profits into the Lynton & Barnstaple Railway project. In October 2005 ownership was transferred to the Milky Way Farm Park.

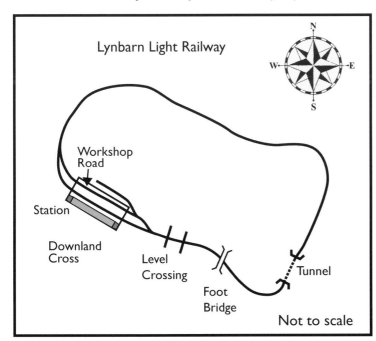

XXVI. This is a rough sketch to show the route that the line followed when visited in 2004. (M.Dart/S.Parkinson)

94. Alan Keefe steam-outline diesel Sir George awaits passengers at Downland Cross on 30th October 2004 before commencing a circuit of the line around some of the grounds of the Farm Park. The locomotive is works no.12 and was built in 1984. (M.Dart)

95. *Downland Cross station was also the line's workshop and it was served by a track alongside the platform road. Undergoing overhaul on 30th October 2004 was this diesel which had operated on the Southport Pier Railway. This locomotive has been rebuilt and is in operation. At the rear of the locomotive is Lynton & Barnstaple Railway covered van no.27. (M.Dart)*

——————→ **96.** *Also on the workshop road on the same date was steam-outline 0-4-0D* Parracombe *which was Baguley works no. 3232 of 1947. (M.Dart)*

——————→ **97.** *Sir George has departed from Downland Cross and is about to pass over a level crossing on 30th October 2004. This crossing was fully protected by warning bells interlocked with the barriers and signal. Immediately beyond the crossing, the line passed under a bridge before entering a short tunnel. Unfortunately it proved impossible to access a location to record the train entering or leaving the tunnel. The route can be seen skirting a planted enclosure, which formed a maze for the entertainment of visitors. The workshop line was fitted with doors at each end. (M.Dart)*

LYNTON & BARNSTAPLE RAILWAY

A group was formed in the early 1980s with the intention of gradually relaying and reopening the line which closed to passengers in 1935. Parcels of land have been gradually acquired and in 2000 the site of Woody Bay station was purchased. Clearance and track laying westwards from there commenced and stock arrived during September 2001. Limited passengers operations on the 2ft gauge line commenced during 2004 and the line was gradually extended in sections. Rolling stock awaiting restoration was stabled on track at the site of Chelfham station where the listed viaduct has been renovated. The railway has a non-rail connected workshop in the village of Bratton Fleming.

➡ **98.** **We are at Lynton station on 9th September 2005 where the original building forms a backdrop. The track bed has been filled in and grassed over but the platform edge is still defined. The station is a private residence and on the lawn is this 2ft gauge Ruston & Hornsby diesel locomotive awaiting restoration. The loco is owned by W.L.A.Pryor and is no.3 and was named** *Brunel.* **Built in 1936, it is works number 179880. The railway is hoping to return to this station in the future.(M.Dart)**

XXVII.   This shows the layout in 2006. (M.Dart/S.Parkinson)

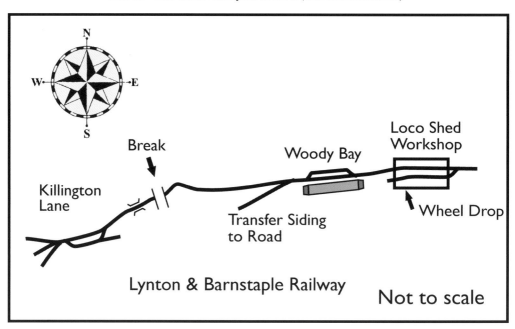

➡ **99.** **Now we move to the restored Woody Bay station on the same day where the weather became very inclement. This is the headquarters of the reopened line and the train at the platform is awaiting departure, hauled by 4wDM** *Holwell Castle.* **The locomotive has the works no.11117 and is a Motor Rail product that dates from July 1961.The locomotive shed is in the background. (M.Dart)**

100. *Inside the locomotive shed on the same day was another Motor Rail 4wDM* Titch. *This was built in 1941 with works no. 8729. The locomotive shed also houses a small museum of various station names and station signs. (M.Dart)*

101. *This is Hunslet 4WD* Exmoor Ranger *inside the shed during the same visit. This locomotive which dates from 1993 was rebuilt by Vane-Tempest. (M.Dart)*

102. *It has rained on every visit made by the author to this railway and 30th December 2006 was no exception when 0-6-0WT* Bronllwyd *was in use. It was being serviced after working trains to Killington Lane and back. This locomotive has works no. 1743 and was built by Hudswell Clarke in 1930. (M.Dart)*

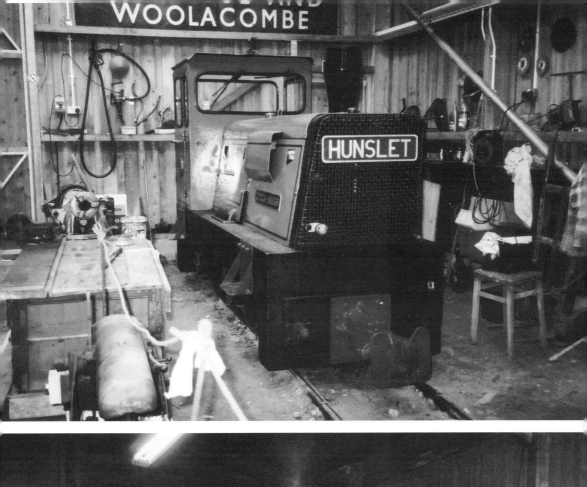

103. Standing outside the shed on the same day was Hunslet diesel Heddon Hall. *(M.Dart)*

104.   Now we look west from Woody Bay on 11th September 2004 shortly after the first section of the line had been reopened. Spoil wagons stand in a siding on the left, whilst other construction materials are ranged alongside the track on the right. The running line falls gently and the transfer siding climbs to the left towards a driveway from the main road. This siding is used to deliver construction and other material to the line. (M.Dart)

105.   During the visit on 9th September 2005, three items of rolling stock were at the top end of the transfer siding. A well wagon is carrying timber and a small open wagon is loaded with ballast. The bogie open wagon is loaded with a delivery of coal for the steam locomotive. (M.Dart)

106.   Work was still in progress at the west end of the line. We look east at Killington Lane on 23rd February 2007 and see 4wD *Heddon Hall* at the platform with an engineers train. This location was the limit of operations. The line descending on the right is on the alignment that leads to Parracombe which constitutes the next extension. (M.Dart)

107.   *Bronllwyd* has run around the train at Killington Lane and is waiting to be coupled prior to returning to Woody Bay on 30th December 2006. Heavy rain enhanced the steam effectively. The guard is giving the driver the signal to stop. (M.Dart)

108. *Minutes before the previous photograph was taken,* Bronllwyd *had backed off its train to enter the shunting neck at the west end of Killington Lane and was running forward to pass along the loop. A spoil wagon and construction items are in the sidings. When the extension to Parracombe has been opened, it is planned to establish a construction and engineering depot here. (M.Dart)*

109.   The line will eventually be re-opened to Bratton Fleming, which was the third station west of the present terminus. At the top of this village, remote from the line, the railway has extensive workshop facilities for the overhaul of locomotives and rolling stock. During a visit to the line by members of the Cornwall Railway Society on 11th September 2004 the Works was visited. Motor Rail diesel *Heddon Hall* was undergoing refurbishment. (M.Dart)

110.   Several miles west of Bratton Fleming the route of the line reaches Chelfham where the station house is extant at the east end of the restored viaduct. The railway owns the station and surrounding area and numerous items of rolling stock are stored on lengths of track awaiting restoration. This site was also visited on 11th September 2004. (M.Dart)

LYNTON & LYNMOUTH CLIFF RAILWAY

This line of 3ft 9in gauge was authorised in 1888 and opened on Easter Monday 1890. Financed by Sir George Newnes, it has a length of 862ft and is on a gradient of 1 in 1 ¾. The gain in height vertically is 500ft. Each car has a tank below its floor, which is filled with water at Lynton at the top end. On arrival at Lynmouth at the foot, most of the water is discharged from the tank and the car is ready to ascend, pulled by the heavier descending car. Water extracted from the West Lyn River is piped to a reservoir. The cars are connected to a continuous cable which passes around pulley wheels of 6ft diameter at the top and bottom. Two independent braking systems ensure absolute safety. The bodies of the cars are removable to permit the carriage of seaborne goods and at times, motor vehicles. The railway's route passed through the grounds of the North Cliff Hotel and the owner of the hotel was compensated by constructing a private platform for the use of hotel guests and staff. It was last used in the 1960s, but on 24th July 2004, by arrangement, it was used to transport a Bridegroom and his best man from the hotel to Lynton.

Further photographs of this line may be found in Branch Line to Lynton.

---

111.   This undated photograph shows a car at Lynton station about to commence the descent to Lynmouth. Passengers board the car from the small platform seen to the left of centre and exit through the small gate in front of the car. Part of the Tea Room is seen on the right. (Lynton & Lynmouth Cliff Railway)

112.   This view from the early 1900s looks up the cliff railway from a point above the lower station at Lynmouth. Several bridges cross the route of the line and part of the North Cliff Hotel can be seen at the top centre. The second passenger car is just beyond the top bridge. Note the signal bell hanging on a post at the bottom.
(Photochrom Co Ltd)

113.   We see the lower station at Lynmouth on 3rd November 1997 with a passenger car waiting to commence the ascent to Lynton. The post supports the entrance arch. The main road along the village is immediately behind the photographer. (M.Dart)

MORWELLHAM QUAY MINE TRAMWAY

The ancient port of Morwellham was on the east bank of the River Tamar above Calstock and had fallen into disuse by 1890, following the demise of the surrounding copper and arsenic mines. The site became very overgrown and derelict. Around June 1970 work commenced to gradually undertake the restoration of the historical site. The George & Charlotte copper mine was south of the port. The mine was renovated and a new adit was constructed to permit entry to the ground level section, which opened to the public in August 1978. Access to the mine was by means of a 2ft gauge railway which was 1100yd in length. The line skirts the bank of the river and enters the mine. After several stops inside to view displays, the train leaves the mine and terminates at the site of another old village called New Quay. Return is along the riverbank to rejoin the outward route.

XXVIII.   This sketch shows the line running from south of the quays at Morwellham into the mine and emerging to arrive at New Quay. It returns along the riverbank. (M.Dart/S.Parkinson)

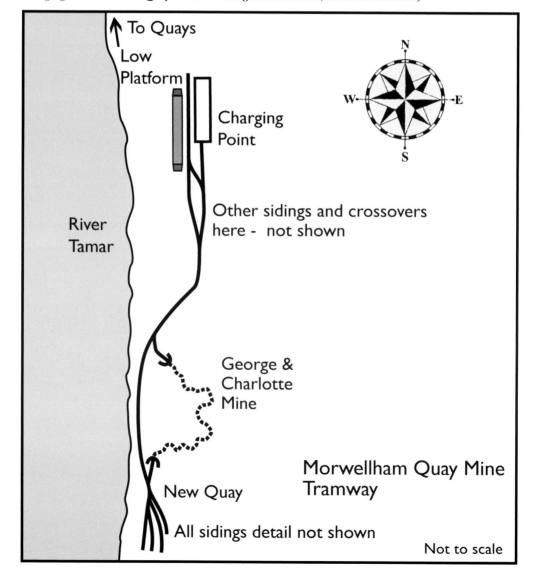

114.   We look south at the terminal station at Morwellham Quay on 24th July 2006, as 4w battery electric locomotive *Ludo* has arrived back from New Quay on the last train of the day. The locomotive has been uncoupled ready to move forward to the charging station. The notice warning passengers to 'mind your head' is necessary, as boarding commences at the rear end of the train and passengers have to duck as they walk through the carriages. Spare sets of carriages and locos are stabled on the right hand line nearest to the riverbank. *(M.Dart)*

115.   On the same date battery locomotive *Bertha* approaches the terminus at Morwellham Quay with a good load of visitors. It is passing two rakes of carriages between which battery loco *Mary* is stabled. *(M.Dart)*

116.   We are a little to the north of the terminus at New Quay on the same date. Battery locomotive *Ludo* is bringing a train load of visitors out from the George & Charlotte mine. Spoil wagons are usually to be found in the sidings at this end of the line. They are used on maintenance trains especially within the mine. After the loco has run around at New Quay the train will return to Morwellham Quay along the line on the left that skirts the riverbank. (M.Dart)

117.	Again on the same day, we look south to the terminus at New Quay. Battery loco *Mary* has arrived in the engineers sidings, as *Ludo* departs on a train to Morwellham Quay. At present there is no passenger station at New Quay. Part of a lifting gantry is on the left. (M.Dart)

118.	We have left New Quay and are walking back north along the riverside route to Morwellham on the same date. The lineside mirror, notices and check rail are of interest. (M.Dart

2 m.p.h.
SOUND
BELL

BEWARE
TRAINS

POWDERHAM CASTLE RAILWAY

This was a line of 1ft 3in gauge which opened during August 2001 to carry visitors to a remote part of the grounds. It ran for between one third and half of a mile but due to problems with the steam locomotive it operated only very intermittently. The locomotive was a facsimile of a GWR Dukedog numbered 3205 named Earl of Devon. After continuing problems with the engine, the line closed after a few weeks. The track was removed and the locomotive was sold for scrap. A miniature line has subsequently been laid on part of the formation.

———————→ **119.** *This was the scene at the terminus at the castle end of the line on 9th September 2001. The line's two carriages stand alongside the rudimentary wooden platform. A lifting gantry spanned the line leading to the shed, which contained the locomotive. (M.Dart)*

XXIX. Final track diagram.

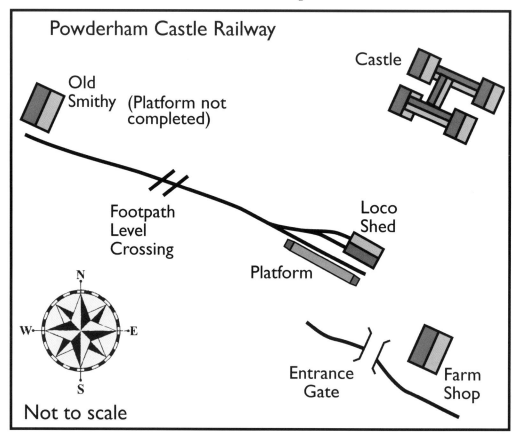

———————→ **120.** *Replica GWR Dukedog class 4-4-0 no. 3205* Earl of Devon, **built by Prestige Engineering Ltd in 2001, has arrived at the Old Smithy terminus of the Powderham Castle Railway on 7th April 2002. Plans to use the area on the right to lay a run-round loop and to construct a platform did not come to fruition. The 15 inch gauge line closed early in 2003 and the track was lifted. A miniature line of 7¼ inch gauge was laid during 2004. This was also unsuccessful and closed at the end of June 2006. The track was lifted by the end of August 2006. (S.Mortimer)**

Middleton Press

EVOLVING THE ULTIMATE RAIL ENCYCLOPEDIA

Easebourne Lane, Midhurst, West Sussex.
GU29 9AZ Tel:01730 813169

www.middletonpress.co.uk   email:info@middletonpress.co.uk

A-0 906520   B-1 873793   C-1 901706   D-1 904474

OOP Out of print at time of printing - Please check availability   BROCHURE AVAILABLE SHOWING NEW TITLES

A
Abergavenny to Merthyr C 91 8
Abertillery and Ebbw Vale Lines D 84 5
Aldgate & Stepney Tramways B 70 1
Allhallows - Branch Line to A 62 8
Alton - Branch Lines to A 11 6
Andover to Southampton A 82 6
Ascot - Branch Lines around A 64 2
Ashburton - Branch Line to B 95 4
Ashford - Steam to Eurostar B 67 1
Ashford to Dover A 48 2
Austrian Narrow Gauge D 04 3
Avonmouth - BL around D 42 5
Aylesbury to Rugby D 91 3
B
Baker Street to Uxbridge D 90 6
Banbury to Birmingham D 27 2
Barking to Southend C 80 2
Barnet & Finchley Tramways B 93 0
Barry - Branch Lines around D 50 0
Basingstoke to Salisbury A 89 5
Bath Green Park to Bristol C 36 9
Bath to Evercreech Junction A 60 4
Bath Tramways B 86 2
Battle over Portsmouth 1940 A 29 1
Battle over Sussex 1940 A 79 6
Bedford to Wellingborough D 31 9
Betwixt Petersfield & Midhurst A 94 9
Bletchley to Cambridge D 94 4
Bletchley to Rugby E 07 9
Blitz over Sussex 1941-42 B 35 0
Bodmin - Branch Lines around B 83 1
Bognor at War 1939-45 B 59 6
Bombers over Sussex 1943-45 B 51 0
Bournemouth & Poole Trys B 47 3
Bournemouth to Evercreech Jn A 46 8
Bournemouth to Weymouth A 57 4
Bournemouth Trolleybuses C 10 9
Bradford Trolleybuses D 19 7
Brecon to Neath D 43 2
Brecon to Newport D 16 6
Brecon to Newtown E 06 2
Brickmaking in Sussex B 19 0
Brightons Tramways B 02 2 OOP
Brighton to Eastbourne A 16 1
Brighton to Worthing A 03 1
Brighton Trolleybuses D 34 0
Bristols Tramways B 57 2
Bristol to Taunton D 03 6
Bromley South to Rochester B 23 7
Bromsgrove to Birmingham D 87 6
Bromsgrove to Gloucester D 73 9
Brunel - A railtour of his achievements D 74 6
Bude - Branch Line to B 29 9
Burnham to Evercreech Jn A 68 0
Burton & Ashby Tramways C 51 2
C
Camberwell & West Norwood Tys B 22 0
Cambridge to Ely D 55 5
Canterbury - Branch Lines around B 58 9
Cardiff Trolleybuses D 64 7
Caterham & Tattenham Corner B 25 1
Changing Midhurst C 15 4
Chard and Yeovil - BLs around C 30 7
Charing Cross to Dartford A 75 8
Charing Cross to Orpington A 96 3
Cheddar - Branch Line to B 90 9
Cheltenham to Andover C 43 7
Cheltenham to Redditch D 81 4
Chesterfield Tramways D 37 1
Chesterfield Trolleybuses D 51 7
Chester Tramways E 04 8
Chichester to Portsmouth A 14 7
Clapham & Streatham Trys B 97 8
Clapham Junction - 50 yrs C 06 2 OOP
Clapham Junction to Beckenham Jn B 36 7
Clevedon & Portishead - BLs to D 18 0
Collectors Trains, Trolleys & Trams D 29 6
Colonel Stephens D62 3
Cornwall Narrow Gauge D 56 2
Cowdray & Easebourne D 96 8
Crawley to Littlehampton A 34 5
Cromer - Branch Lines around A 26 6
Croydons Tramways B 42 8
Croydons Trolleybuses B 73 2 OOP
Croydon to East Grinstead B 48 0
Crystal Palace (HL) & Catford Loop A 87 1
D
Darlington to Newcastle D 98 2
Darlington Trolleybuses D 33 3
Dartford to Sittingbourne B 34 3
Derby Tramways D 17 3
Derby Trolleybuses C 72 7
Derwent Valley - Branch Line to the D 06 7
Devon Narrow Gauge E 09 3
Didcot to Banbury D 02 9
Didcot to Swindon C 84 0
Didcot to Winchester C 13 0
Dorset & Somerset Narrow Gauge D 76 0
Douglas to Peel C 88 8

Douglas to Port Erin C 55 0
Douglas to Ramsey D 39 5
Dovers Tramways B 24 4
Dover to Ramsgate A 78 9
E
Ealing to Slough C 42 0
Eastbourne to Hastings A 27 7 OOP
East Cornwall Mineral Railways D 22 7
East Croydon to Three Bridges A 53 6
East Grinstead - Branch Lines to A 07 9
East Ham & West Ham Tramways B 52 7
East Kent Light Railway A 61 1 OOP
East London - Branch Lines of C 44 4
East London Line B 80 0
East Ridings Secret Resistance D 21 0
Edgware & Willesden Tramways C 18 5
Effingham Junction - BLs around A 74 1
Eltham & Woolwich Tramways B 74 9 OOP
Ely to Kings Lynn C 53 6
Ely to Norwich C 90 1
Embankment & Waterloo Tramways B 41 1
Enfield & Wood Green Trys C 03 1 OOP
Enfield Town & Palace Gates - BL to D 32 6
Epsom to Horsham A 30 7
Euston to Harrow & Wealdstone C 89 5
Exeter & Taunton Tramways B 32 9
Exeter to Barnstable B 15 2
Exeter to Newton Abbot C 49 9
Exeter to Tavistock B 69 5
Exmouth - Branch Lines to B 00 8
F
Fairford - Branch Line to A 52 9
Falmouth, Helston & St. Ives - BL to C 74 1
Fareham to Salisbury A 67 3
Faversham to Dover B 05 3
Felixstowe & Aldeburgh - BL to D 20 3
Fenchurch Street to Barking C 20 8
Festiniog - 50 yrs of enterprise C 83 3
Festiniog 1946-55 E 01 7 - PUB 21 APRIL
Festiniog in the Fifties B 68 8
Festiniog in the Sixties B 91 6
Finsbury Park to Alexandra Palace C 02 4
Frome to Bristol B 77 0
Fulwell - Trams, Trolleys & Buses D 11 1
G
Gloucester to Bristol D 35 7
Gloucester to Cardiff D 66 1
Gosport & Horndean Trys B 92 3
Gosport - Branch Lines around A 36 9
Great Yarmouth Tramways D 13 5
Greece Narrow Gauge D 72 2
Greenwich & Dartford Tramways B 14 5 OOP
Grimsby & Cleethorpes Trolleybuses D 86 9
Guildford to Redhill A 63 5 OOP
H
Hammersmith & Hounslow Trys C 33 8
Hampshire Narrow Gauge D 36 4
Hampshire Waterways A 84 0 OOP
Hampstead & Highgate Tramways B 53 4
Harrow to Watford D 14 2
Hastings to Ashford A 37 6
Hastings Tramways B 18 3
Hastings Trolleybuses B 81 7 OOP
Hawkhurst - Branch Line to A 66 6
Hay-on-Wye - Branch Lines around D 92 0
Hayling - Branch Line to A 12 3
Haywards Heath to Seaford A 28 4
Hemel Hempstead - Branch Lines to D 88 3
Henley, Windsor & Marlow - BL to C77 2
Hereford to Newport D 54 8
Hexham to Carlisle D 75 3
Hitchin to Peterborough D 07 4
Holborn & Finsbury Tramways B 79 4
Holborn Viaduct to Lewisham A 81 9
Horsham - Branch Lines to A 02 4
Huddersfield Tramways D 95 1
Huddersfield Trolleybuses C 92 5
Hull Tramways D60 9
Hull Trolleybuses D 24 1
Huntingdon - Branch Lines around A 93 2
I
Ilford & Barking Tramways B 61 9
Ilford to Shenfield C 97 0
Ilfracombe - Branch Line to B 21 3
Ilkeston & Glossop Tramways D 40 1
Industrial Rlys of the South East A 09 3
Ipswich to Saxmundham C 41 3
Ipswich Trolleybuses D 59 3
Isle of Wight Lines - 50 yrs C 12 3
K
Keighley Tramways & Trolleybuses D 83 8
Kent & East Sussex Waterways A 72 X
Kent Narrow Gauge C 45 1
Kent Seaways - Hoys to Hovercraft D 79 1
Kidderminster to Shrewsbury E10 9
Kingsbridge - Branch Line to C 98 7
Kingston & Hounslow Loops A 83 3 OOP
Kingston & Wimbledon Tramways B 56 5
Kingswear - Branch Line to C 17 8

L
Lambourn - Branch Line to C 70 3
Launceston & Princetown - BL to C 19 2
Lewisham & Catford Tramways B 26 8 OOP
Lewisham to Dartford A 92 5
Lines around Wimbledon B 75 6
Liverpool Street to Chingford D 01 2
Liverpool Street to Ilford C 34 5
Liverpool Tramways - Eastern C 04 8
Liverpool Tramways - Northern C 46 8
Liverpool Tramways - Southern C 23 9
London Bridge to Addiscombe B 20 6
London Bridge to East Croydon A 58 1
London Chatham & Dover Railway A 88 8
London Termini - Past and Proposed D 00 5
London to Portsmouth Waterways B 43 5
Longmoor - Branch Lines to A 41 3
Looe - Branch Line to A 80 2
Lyme Regis - Branch Line to A 45 1
Lynton - Branch Line to B 04 6
M
Maidstone & Chatham Tramways B 40 4
Maidstone Trolleybuses C 00 0 OOP
March - Branch Lines around B 09 1
Margate & Ramsgate Tramways C 52 9
Marylebone to Rickmansworth D49 4
Melton Constable to Yarmouth Beach E 03 1
Midhurst - Branch Lines around A 49 9
Midhurst - Branch Lines to A 01 7 OOP
Military Defence of West Sussex A 23 9
Military Signals, South Coast C 54 3
Minehead - Branch Line to A 80 2
Mitcham Junction Lines B 01 5
Mitchell & company C 59 8
Monmouthshire Eastern Valleys D 71 5
Moreton-in-Marsh to Worcester D 26 5
Moretonhampstead - BL to C 27 7
Mountain Ash to Neath D 80 7
N
Newbury to Westbury C 66 6
Newcastle to Hexham D 98 2
Newcastle Trolleybuses D 78 4
Newport (IOW) - Branch Lines to A 26 0
Newquay - Branch Lines to C 71 0
Newton Abbot to Plymouth C 60 4
Northern France Narrow Gauge C 75 8
North East German Narrow Gauge D 44 9
North Kent Tramways B 44 2
North London Line B 94 7
North Woolwich - BLs around C 65 9
Norwich Tramways C 40 6
Nottinghamshire & Derbyshire T/B D 63 0
Nottinghamshire & Derbyshire T/W D 53 1
O
Ongar - Branch Lines to E 05 5
Orpington to Tonbridge B 03 9 OOP
Oxford to Bletchley D57 9
Oxford to Moreton-in-Marsh D 15 9
P
Paddington to Ealing C 37 5
Paddington to Princes Risborough C 81 9
Padstow - Branch Line to B 54 1
Plymouth - BLs around B 98 5
Plymouth to St. Austell C 63 5
Pontypool to Mountain Ash D 65 4
Porthmadog 1954-94 - BL around B 31 2
Porthmadog to Blaenau B 50 3 OOP
Portmadoc 1923-46 - BL around B 13 8
Portsmouths Tramways B 72 5
Portsmouth to Southampton A 31 4
Portsmouth Trolleybuses C 73 4
Potters Bar to Cambridge D 70 8
Princes Risborough - Branch Lines to D 05 0
Princes Risborough to Banbury C 85 7
R
Railways to Victory C 16 1 OOP
Reading to Basingstoke B 27 5
Reading to Didcot C 79 7
Reading to Guildford A 47 5 OOP
Reading Tramways B 87 9
Reading Trolleybuses C 05 5
Redhill to Ashford A 73 4
Return to Blaenau 1970-82 C 64 2
Rickmansworth to Aylesbury D 61 6
Roman Roads of Hampshire D 67 8
Roman Roads of Kent E 02 4
Roman Roads of Surrey C 61 1
Roman Roads of Sussex C 48 2
Romneyrail C 32 1
Ryde to Ventnor A 19 2
S
Salisbury to Westbury B 39 8
Salisbury to Yeovil B 06 0 OOP
Saxmundham to Yarmouth C 69 7
Saxony Narrow Gauge D 47 0
Seaton & Eastbourne Tramways B 76 3 OOP
Seaton & Sidmouth - Branch Lines to A 95 6
Secret Sussex Resistance B 82 6
SECR Centenary album C 11 6
Selsey - Branch Line to A 04 8

Sheerness - Branch Lines around B 16 9
Shepherds Bush to Uxbridge T/Ws C 28 4
Shrewsbury - Branch Line to A 86 4
Sierra Leone Narrow Gauge D 28 9
Sirhowy Valley Line E 12 3
Sittingbourne to Ramsgate A 90 1
Slough to Newbury C 56 7
Solent - Creeks, Crafts & Cargoes D 52 4
Southamptons Tramways B 33 6
Southampton to Bournemouth A 42 0
Southend-on-Sea Tramways B 28 2
Southern France Narrow Gauge C 47 5
Southwark & Deptford Tramways B 38 1
Southwold - Branch Line to A 15 4
South Eastern & Chatham Railways C 08 6
South London Line B 46 6
South London Tramways 1903-33 D 10 4
South London Tramways 1933-52 D 89 0
St. Albans to Bedford D 08 1
St. Austell to Penzance C 67 3
St. Pancras to Barking D 68 5
St. Pancras to St. Albans C 78 9
Stamford Hill Tramways B 85 5
Steaming through Cornwall B 30 5 OOP
Steaming through Kent A 13 0 OOP
Steaming through the Isle of Wight A 56 7
Steaming through West Hants A 69 7
Stratford upon avon to Birmingham D 77 7
Stratford upon Avon to Cheltenham C 25 3
Strood to Paddock Wood B 12 1 OOP
Surrey Home Guard C 57 4
Surrey Narrow Gauge C 87 1
Surrey Waterways A 51 2 OOP
Sussex Home Guard C 24 6
Sussex Narrow Gauge C 68 0
Sussex Shipping Sail, Steam & Motor D 23 4
Swanley to Ashford B 45 9
Swindon to Bristol C 96 3
Swindon to Gloucester D46 3
Swindon to Newport D 30 2
Swiss Narrow Gauge C 94 9
T
Talyllyn - 50 years C 39 0
Taunton to Barnstaple B 60 2
Taunton to Exeter C 82 6
Tavistock to Plymouth B 88 6
Tees-side Trolleybuses D 58 6
Tenterden - Branch Line to A 21 5
Thanets Tramways B 11 4 OOP
Three Bridges to Brighton A 35 2
Tilbury Loop C 86 4
Tiverton - Branch Lines around C 62 8
Tivetshall to Beccles D 41 8
Tonbridge to Hastings A 44 4
Torrington - Branch Lines to B 37 4
Tunbridge Wells - Branch Lines to A 32 1
Twickenham & Kingston Trys C 35 2
Two-Foot Gauge Survivors C 21 5 OOP
U
Upwell - Branch Line to B 64 0
V
Victoria & Lambeth Tramways B 49 7
Victoria to Bromley South A 98 7
Victoria to East Croydon A 40 6 OOP
Vivarais C 31 4 OOP
Vivarais Revisited E 08 6
W
Walthamstow & Leyton Tramways B 65 7
Waltham Cross & Edmonton Trys C 07 9
Wandsworth & Battersea Tramways B 63 3
Wantage - Branch Line to D 25 8
Wareham to Swanage - 50 yrs D 09 8
War on the Line A 10 9
War on the Line VIDEO + 88 0
Waterloo to Windsor A 54 3
Waterloo to Woking A 38 3
Watford to Leighton Buzzard D 45 6
Wenford Bridge to Fowey C 09 3
Westbury to Bath B 55 8
Westbury to Taunton C 76 5
West Cornwall Mineral Railways D 48 7
West Croydon to Epsom B 08 4
West German Narrow Gauge D 93 7
West London - Branch Lines of C 50 5
West London Line B 84 8
West Sussex Waterways A 24 6 OOP
West Wiltshire - Branch Lines of D 12 8
Weymouth - Branch Lines around A 65 9
Willesden Junction to Richmond B 71 8
Wimbledon to Beckenham C 58 1
Wimbledon to Epsom B 62 6
Wimborne - Branch Lines around A 97 0
Wisbech - Branch Lines around C 01 7
Wisbech 1800-1901 C 93 2
Woking to Alton A 59 8
Woking to Portsmouth A 25 3
Woking to Southampton A 55 0
Wolverhampton Trolleybuses D 85 2
Woolwich & Dartford Trolleys B 66 4
Worcester to Birmingham D 97 5
Worcester to Hereford D 38 8
Worthing to Chichester A 06 2
Y
Yeovil - 50 yrs change C 38 3
Yeovil to Dorchester A 76 5 OOP
Yeovil to Exeter A 91 8
York Tramways & Trolleybuses D 82 1